INDEX
ON CENSORSHIP

INDEX ON CENSORSHIP 5 1999

WEBSITE NEWS UPDATED WEEKLY
www.indexoncensorship.org
contact@indexoncensorship.org
tel: 0171-278 2313
fax: 0171-278 1878

Volume 28 No 5 September/October 1999 Issue 190

Index on Censorship (ISSN 0306-4220) is published bi-monthly by a non-profit-making company: Writers & Scholars International Ltd, Lancaster House, 33 Islington High Street, London N1 9LH. *Index on Censorship* is associated with Writers & Scholars Educational Trust, registered charity number 325003
Periodicals postage: (US subscribers only) paid at Newark, New Jersey. Postmaster: send US address changes to *Index on Censorship* c/o Mercury Airfreight International Ltd Inc, 365 Blair Road, Avenel, NJ 07001, USA
© This selection Writers & Scholars International Ltd, London 1999
© Contributors to this issue, except where otherwise indicated

Subscriptions (6 issues per annum)
Individuals: UK £39, US $52, rest of world £45
Institutions: UK £44, US $80, rest of world £50
Speak to Tony Callaghan on 0171 278 2313

EDITORIAL

Untidy new world

The first real sign came in Poland in April, when Solidarity was allowed to contest elections. Then, in May, Hungarian border troops pulled down the barbed-wire frontier with Austria. In June there was the brutality of Tiananmen Square in Beijing. In August Polish communism ended with the election of Tadeusz Mazowiecki. In October East Germans streamed to the West through the open Hungarian-Austrian border. On 9 November, bewildered guards let East Berliners through the Wall, and that night Ossies and Wessies began to tear down their 28-year-old monster. The year was 1989: it was the start of a huge wave of revolution, unforeseen and dramatic, that would eventually sweep away the entire Soviet Empire – so synonymous for us in the West with censorship.

There were other milestones.1989 was also the year when the Russians left Afghanistan (p66), when Slobodan Milosevic made his historic speech insisting that Kosovo was part of Serbia and removing its autonomous status, when President Botha met Nelson Mandela in prison.

So where are we, 10 years on? *Index* explores a world which, without the constraints imposed by the Cold War, has become less orderly, where nationalism, enlightened as well as authoritarian, is part of everyone's consciousness (p181), and has been the force behind many of the decade's wars (p92); where religious fanaticism is often in conflict with modernisation (p48); where the Internet has created new freedoms – and spawned new attempts to suppress them (p106); and where tough free market policies and globalisation (p111) have more or less demolished the rights of workers and made the divisions between rich and poor ever larger. There's no sign of the peace dividend, and some might argue that the right side (communism) lost the Cold War the wrong side (unfettered capitalism) won. Meanwhile the old liberal, secular consensus in India may be breaking down (p72), the Chinese Communist Party survives (p81), the USA has embraced a triumphalist ideology (p41) and, in some countries (though not Ireland nor Israel), truth and reconciliation commissions have grappled painfully with their brutal histories.

In 1989 people fought for freedom. What they got was democracy. And democracy, as Hans Magnus Enzensburger once remarked, is 'where the dirt comes out'. Is there hope of some order out of the new chaos? The setting up of the International Criminal Court (p170), giving an international community the right to intervene in sovereign states in the name of human rights, could, with luck, help shape the 21st century. At least the past decade could then pass gracefully into history. ❏

contents

LETTERS

Human rights are universal
From Ian Ellis, Menstrie

Carl Stotton's letter (*Index* 4/99) describes clearly why journals of social conscience such as yours are vital in our society. This letter is nothing more than a rationalisation or disguise of prejudice. It is the sort of reasoning which can be used to dehumanise anybody in any section of society. It is precisely his reasoning – that some people do not deserve the same human rights as the rest of us – which was used by the Nazis when they tried to exterminate people they did not like.

The wrong kind of censorship?
From Tom Blair, Pennsylvania

I just received my first issue of *Index on Censorship*. I must say I am very disappointed. I had hoped your journal would put the principle of freedom of speech above the usual political agenda but you don't.

Did it ever occur to you that left-wing governments are just as capable of censorship as right-wing? Did it ever occur to you that believers in globalism, secularism and rationalism are just as capable of censorship as nationalists and monotheists?

The reason I bring this up is because now more than any time in my 51 years we are seeing left-wing censorship throughout the West. We now have laws against certain types of speech and writing and imprisonment of violators in England, France, Germany, Austria, Spain and Belgium. We see fines levied against journalists in Canada. We are seeing legal proscriptions against Internet sites in America. We have laws passed against certain types of political expression in Russia, Canada, and Europe. All of these actions are taken by so-called democratic governments. The speech I am referring to usually centres around WWII history, racial nationalism, anti-globalism, and some cases Christian, Islamic or pagan religious speech.

The right to freedom from offence and the right to freedom of expression are *mutually incompatible*. The latter is what is being called a 'human right' today – but you publish under the guise of opposing censorship. I think you need to decide what you stand for and be honest about it. To the extent you do decide to stand for freedom of expression, then you should protect the people from the government – not vice versa.

I see no reason to subscribe to a periodical that gives me the same articles I could read in the *New York Times* or the *Washington Post*. Let me know when you write serious articles in support of Robert Fourisson, Doug Collins, David Irving, Ernst Zundel, Dr Ingred Rimland, Gerhad Forster, Udo Walendy etc. Until then, please cancel my subscription. You misrepresented yourselves in your advertisement. ❏

NILOU MOBASSER

Date with destiny

It is 10 years since Ayatollah Khomeini died and he might not recognise his revolution today. But as recent events have shown, it is the Iranian people who will decide its future

Iranians have always had a propensity for dates. Everyone is expected to know, for example, what Shahrivar 1320 (1941) means, even if they were born years after the day when Allied troops marched into and occupied Iran. And you can hardly claim to be Iranian at all if you don't know 28 Mordad, the date of the US-backed coup in 1953 against the much-loved prime minister Mohammad Mosaddeq.

The 1979 revolution, too, has produced its own armoury of dates. There is 13 Aban, for example, the day of the takeover of the US embassy in Tehran – seen in a way as a riposte to 28 Mordad. And it is hardly possible to carry on a conversation about Iranian politics these days without mentioning 2 Khordad, the day Mohammad Khatami was elected president against the odds in 1997.

In the early hours of Friday 9 July 1999 on the western calendar, another date was stamped on the Iranian psyche: 18 Tir. On this date, law enforcement forces accompanied by other, unidentified men stormed a Tehran University dormitory, savagely attacked half-asleep students and transformed their tiny, sparsely equipped rooms into gutted bomb sites. Why? Rightly or wrongly Khatami stands for something in Iran. He stands for the strength and the will of the people who elected him when they were expected to go to the polling stations like sheep to vote for someone else. He symbolises people's burgeoning interest in raising their voice and speaking for themselves. He stands for a nascent trend in Iran of calling a spade a spade. And most significantly – as far as understanding 18 Tir is concerned – he represents the current determination of the people to change their society without rancour or

Iranian students gather in support of President Khatami, Tehran, May 1999 – Credit: Caren Firouz/Reuters

violence.

Iranians have grown up. They take an interest in matters that affect them and their country and feel they are capable of and have a right to shape their own lives. There is a higher literacy rate than ever before and people have become voracious readers of a fantastic – although often besieged – press. They don't just want to change things for the sake of it, they want to change things in a considered way that will allow them to flourish. They want to argue and understand. That is what Khatami represents. Khatami has never claimed to have substantive answers. What he offered during his election campaign was a method or a process. His method or process involves the rule of law, transparency and civil society. The rule of law: because people must function within a recognised framework. They must play the game by a defined set of rules. And if they don't like those rules, they must try to change them by the agreed methods. Transparency: because everyone must know where everyone else stands and what interests they represent. Civil society: because it is made up of the political parties, trade unions and other associations and organisations that are the foundation stone of a modern, pluralistic society. People voted for Khatami and against his rivals because they agreed with his method.

Khatami's opponents believe in a different method. Theirs is the method of shameless power and brute force. It is the method of burning bookshops and attacking cinemas. It is the method of locking someone up because you can get away with it and you don't like the way he looks or what he says. It is the method of throwing Molotov cocktails at a newspaper office. It is the method of bundling a writer into a car, strangling him with a piece of rope and throwing his body by a railway track three days later. It is the old, traditional method of power politics. In the midst of all this and in the absence of well-established political parties, it was perhaps inevitable that newspapers would become the front-line of 'the clash of methods'. On the one side, there are the 'traditionalist' publications, with their crudely laid out black-and-white pages, dwelling on every possible failing of Khatami's government, waxing lyrical about all the conspiracies hatched by foreigners and threatening to expose their 'domestic agents and lackeys' who are said to be disguised – wouldn't you know it – as Iranian journalists, intellectuals and even (Khatami's) officials. On the other side of the battle line, there are the colourful array of papers pledging allegiance to 'civil society', tapping a seemingly endless supply of fascinating interviews, debates, editorials, readers' comments and piercing pieces of satire mocking the mindless brutality of the opposition. It was a telling indication of the impact of the attack on the university dormitory that Ebrahim Nabavi, the best-loved satirist of them all, wrote in his column in *Neshat* newspaper the day after 18 Tir that, for the first time since he'd started his column, he was incapable of finding anything to say that could make people laugh. One thing is fairly clear: what happened on 18 Tir was not Khatami's method. And what happened over the next few days in Tehran and other cities was an explosion of anger against the savagery of 18 Tir. But where was Khatami? More than any other section of society, university students had the right to expect Khatami to go to them and to stand by them in their hour of need. They are his power base. They are his constituents. Where was he when they needed him?

Khatami is the president of Iran. He has sworn an oath to uphold the law and the constitution. It is perhaps not the law and the constitution he himself would have chosen but those are the rules of the game and that is his chosen method. He must walk a fine line between upholding the law as it stands and transforming society. He must try to meet the aspirations of the people while exercising the functions of a post that carries very little actual power. He must allow the people to express their anger while hoping it can be directed into constructive channels. It may be years before 18 Tir and the subsequent events are properly analysed and understood to anyone's satisfaction. To this day, people in Iran continue to debate the significance of 28 Mordad and its ramifications. The history of Iran – any more than the history of any other country – cannot be reduced to digestible soundbites. The truth lies beyond such tidy labels as Islamist and secularist, fundamentalist and liberal. The event that immediately preceded the mad attack on the Tehran University dormitory was a gathering on the campus of a few hundred students protesting against the illegal banning of *Salam* newspaper. The paper was immediately labelled 'liberal' by western media. Not so long ago, the managing director of *Salam*, Mohammad Musavi-Kho'ini, was seen as a mentor by the students who stormed the US embassy in Tehran. Heaven only knows what he thinks of being described as a liberal now.

As for Khatami, in the end it will be up to Iranians themselves to decide whether he succeeded or failed. It will be up to them to decide whether he was a liberal or a fundamentalist – and whether it makes any difference to them one way or the other. His constituents are the Iranian people, not western governments. Khatami's pact is with the Iranian people. If they win, he wins. ❏

Nilou Mobasser *is an Iranian writer and translator based in the UK*

MASSOUD BEHNOUD

Fifth time lucky?

The Iranian century is marked by a succession of coups, counter-coups, revolutions and returns to dictatorship. The 1979 revolution produced its own crop of dictators and tyrants, but now, it's time for another go at freedom

My grandmother lost her father in the struggle against dictators during the constitutional revolution in the early years of this century. She herself was forced into a decade-long exile, along with a number of dignitaries from the Qajar dynasty, after the 1921 coup plotted by Britain's General Ironside. My father spent eight years in the notorious Qal'eh Falakol'aflak prison after the 1953 coup against Mossadeq led by the American Kermit Roosevelt. His nephew was killed shouting: 'Death to the American Shah,' during the 1979 revolution against the monarchy.

Most urban middle-class families in Iran carry bitter memories of revolutions and coups that have taken our society to the edge of freedom four times in the course of this century. Dictatorship and repression followed swiftly on each occasion.

Apart from the struggle for freedom, the 20th century is associated in the minds of Iranians with oil, a substance that gushed out of the ground early this century in southern Iran and became the cause of all those coups and hardships because the West was determined to plunder the precious substance. And the dictators acted as their agents. Soon after 1917 Iran became a neighbour of the Soviet Union; the West grew anxious about communist penetration into the oil-rich Persian Gulf area via Iran. Although this constituted a legitimate reason in the eyes of the USA and Europe for backing dictators during the Cold War, Iranians themselves did not see it as sufficient justification for their painful destiny. They came to see foreigners as the cause of all their misfortunes, a view that is hotly debated to this day.

Eight months after the revolution that brought the Shah's dictatorship to an end, the occupation of the US embassy and the holding of 52 Americans as hostages for 444 days was a salve to the anti-western sentiments of Iranian society. But the subsequent conflict between domestic groups heralded a new period of repression and censorship from 1982. This time it was not plotted by foreigners but entirely home-brewed by a State apparatus determined to ensure its own survival. Ironically, it was as if the supporters of the Islamic government who had just emerged from the Shah's prisons were so afraid of another foreign coup, especially one instigated by the USA, that they decided to mount a coup themselves – against freedom. This came as a shock to the Iranian people and did a good deal to raise their consciousness.

The shock was felt most deeply by the younger generation who had played an active role in the Islamic revolution and had paid dearly for its defence, both against counter-revolutionaries and in the eight-year-long war with Iraq. This generation of revolutionary Muslims – the religious intellectuals – was not prepared to see the fruit of its sacrifice transformed into a dictatorial government despised by the people and held in the same kind of low esteem by the international community as the dictatorial regimes imposed by coups. Their determination shaped the current civil movement in Iran that first came to light with its support for Mohammad Khatami in the 1997 presidential election. Khatami succeeded in winning the votes of women and youth, both of whom had endured more than their fair share of pressure and injustice.

The Iranian people's fifth experience of freedom this century was based on a popular, reformist movement and was won through the ballot box, not through the violence and rancour that had proved so ineffective in the past. This movement was resisted from the start by the conservatives and traditionalists who have wielded all the levers of power since 1982. They do not like relinquishing power, submitting to the law or to equality with others and are, therefore, forced to proclaim that freedom and Islam are irreconcilable. They are convinced that, if forced to choose between the two, Muslims will choose religion; the religious intellectuals believe there is no conflict between religion and freedom.

At first, the conservatives tried to impede the civil movement through the law. When this proved ineffective, they resorted to terror and assassination. The killing of Parvaneh and Dariush Forouhar, nationalist leaders opposed to religious tyranny, was followed by the disappearance and murder of at least three freedom-loving writers. As a result of the investigation initiated by the president – with the strong backing of the people – elements at the intelligence ministry were inculpated, a heavy blow to the conservatives. At the same time, the government succeeded in holding the local council elections the conservatives had opposed. The world began to believe in the civil movement in Iran and threw open its doors to the government.

The 15-year-long repression that was imposed on Iran's freedom-lovers from 1982 to 1997, made the new generation of intellectuals aware of a fact that had remained hidden so far. the role played by the people in delaying the civil society that had been heralded since the beginning of the twentieth century with the approval of the constitution. Ali Rezaqoli, the young author of the best-selling book *The Sociology of Elite-icide: a sociological study of some of the causes of tyranny and backwardness in Iran,* first published in Tehran in May 1998 and already in its tenth edition, is not the only one to focus on the part played by the people in perpetuating their own backwardness and repression, and in passively allowing the emergence of dictatorships.

Many now argue that the people must be involved if there is to be any political development; and that freedom of expression and provisions allowing the establishment of political parties and professional associations are essential if this process is to move forward. And it is not the established, traditionally left wing intellectuals who are urging these ideas, but the new generation of religious thinkers. Those of them from within the clerical establishment who have called on their colleagues to join them in this enterprise have been attacked and imprisoned. Khatami's greatest achievement has been to allow these thinkers to emerge and air their views.

The engine of this movement is the younger generation which forms well over half the country's population of 60 million. They want to see the formation of civil society, a free society in which respect for human rights and the aspiration to take its place as a member of the international community are paramount. ❏

Massoud Behnoud is a writer, journalist and documentary film-maker living in Tehran
Translated by Nilou Mobasser

MICHAEL GRIFFIN

Enemy of the people

You'll find a welcome in the Falkland Islands these days – just as long as you don't get too interested in the penguins

After 18 years on the rainswept Lleyn Peninsula in North Wales, biologist Mike Bingham moved to the South Atlantic in October 1993 as conservation officer for Falklands Conservation, a wildlife charity founded by the venerated Sir Peter Scott and funded by the Falkland Islands Government (FIG). Six years on, he is clinging on to the rocks after a nightmare ride through the worst that a remote and largely unaccountable government can throw at an outsider.

In 1995/96 Bingham led a penguin census of the archipelago. The results appeared to reveal a species in deep crisis: the rockhopper penguin population had slumped from over 3 million pairs to less than 300,000. The decline was clearly linked to the boom in squid fishing that has become the Islands' main source of revenue in the 1990s. But with oil exploration fast becoming feasible and 13 companies already expressing interest, environmental objections were the last thing the Islands needed.

In the course of 1996 the nature of Falklands Conservation changed from wildlife club to quasi-government body: FIG councillors and directors of companies involved in oil, fishing and shipping replaced amateur naturalists on the Board of Trustees. DL Clifton, a member of the eight-man Legislative Council established in 1985 after the Falklands War and now a director of Desire Petroleum, one of the companies drilling in the Falklands, became chairman; FIG funding tripled to US$240,000.

In 1996/97, Bingham spent his vacation making a penguin census in South America. He wanted to establish whether the rockhopper decline was a regionwide phenomenon. It was not. On 31 March 1997 he was told by Councillor Clifton that if he did not suppress his findings, he would lose his job, his membership of all FIG committees and be kicked out of the Islands as an 'undesirable'. On 17 April his job was advertised in the local paper, *Penguin News,* and, two months later, he was out: contract terminated.

He determined to go it alone and found shift work at the local power station to pay for further studies under the auspices of his own company, Environmental Research Unit Ltd. His first task was to go public in the pages of *Penguin Conservation* but, by the time the data was published in March 1998, oil exploration was already underway. Falklands Conservation had published rival statistics in the *Atlas of Breeding Birds of the Falkland Islands* in 1997. It recorded 550,000 breeding pairs of rockhopper penguins compared to Bingham's 297,000; and 102,000 breeding pairs of gentoo penguins, not the 65,000 of the 1995/96 census.

Despite criticism from experts, Falklands Conservation continued to publish its controversial figures on the state of the penguin population. In 1998 its annual research report quoted breeding success rates of 1.29 chicks per nest for a species that only rears one egg a year in storm-tossed conditions. Within weeks of the first oil rig arriving in April 1997, three separate oil spills had killed and injured penguins and other seabirds. Despite the fact that gentoos and cormorants forage close to shore, Falklands Conservation claimed the oil had come from outside the 200-mile zone.

Meanwhile, Bingham was seeking funding for his own operation. There were two possible sources: the British Trust for Ornithology (BTO) was interested in an albatross-banding programme and the Islands' Environmental Planning Department (EPD) had written to ask if it could purchase data from his coastline surveys. On 24 April Falklands Conservation wrote to the BTO accusing Bingham of banding birds without a licence and alleged he was also guilty of data theft – although the research that interested the EPD was conducted after his contract had been terminated. On 29 May an FIG official informed him that his application for residency had been suspended because of the charge.

By the time Bingham straightened out these 'misunderstandings' – and Falklands Conservation had sent a full retraction of the charges to FIG – he had lost his funding. FIG refused to lift the block on his residency application, refused to explain why and then refused to reveal the details of the allegations that might have enabled Bingham to take legal action for slander and lost earnings. By now, the shy and retiring local press, in the shape of the *Penguin News*, had become more interested, but FIG refused to talk to the paper.

In September 1998 Bingham's house was broken into. More important than what might have been taken as his discovery of items of a 'highly illegal nature' that had been left behind. On 5 October he told friends that he believed the police or customs were about to search his premises; *Penguin News* now printed a letter and an editorial exposing the campaign against him.

A few days later, customs officers conducting a 'routine mail search' discovered a pornographic video addressed to Bingham from a fictitious name and address in the UK. On 21 November a search of his house duly took place. 'It would all have been very different if I hadn't come across the items hidden under my bed prior to the search,' said Bingham. He was fined for importing prohibited material but not deported.

Then the phone calls began. From the end of January 1999 to March Bingham was subjected to calls threatening further attacks and urging his immediate departure from the Islands. He wrote down every threat and passed the transcripts to the police, his solicitor and the local press. The police signally failed to trace the caller; Bingham became convinced the threats emanated from within the justice system itself. On 21 February he wrote to *Penguin News,* and to the *Sun* and the *Daily Mirror* in the UK, predicting his arrest and further attempts to deport him on false charges.

On 3 March a customs and immigration officer called on him at work to caution him about his possible deportation for alleged deception. Bingham, he claimed, had mentioned no criminal record on his residency application forms, but Falklands police had discovered he had convictions in the UK for burglary, car theft and affray – ample grounds for expulsion. Bingham's fingerprints were dispatched to Interpol. It replied, with considerable irritation, that it had already told the police back in January that the convictions belonged to a man two years older than Bingham and with a different middle name.

On 22 April – one week after the authorities discovered their 'mistake' – Bingham was charged with making a dishonest statement on a job application form. He denied the authenticity of the document in question and, after repeated court appearances, trial was set for 9 August. Two weeks later, Bingham's lawyer was informed by FIG that the case was being withdrawn. 'A week before FIG decided to drop the charges,' said Bingham, 'they notified me in writing that if I insisted on proceeding with a plea of "not guilty" and if I lost the case, an order would be sought to make me pay all the prosecution costs including the cost of witnesses attending. I told them I was prepared to take the risk since I did not believe I could lose. The fact that the attorney general withdrew for fear of being left holding the bill suggests he thought so too.' The Falklands police have now admitted that the application form they presented during Bingham's interview had been fabricated at the police station.

Attempts at redress have fallen on deaf ears. Complaints against the immigration department remain unacknowledged while the Police Complaints Authority in London say that jurisdiction lies with the Islands' governor, who is 'too busy' to see Bingham or to reply to his letters. Meanwhile, the harassment – both official and unofficial – continues: his residency is still suspended, Bingham's wife and son are now receiving malicious calls and, on 16 August, someone sabotaged his vehicle.

So why does he stay in such an inhospitable zone? Though the oil companies have so far not found commercial quantities, drilling is shortly to begin to west of the Falklands, the most sensitive wildlife area. 'At present,' explains Bingham, 'there is a cosy arrangement whereby the FIG pays Falklands Conservation large sums of money and, in exchange, it supports government policy, even to the detriment of the wildlife they are sworn to protect. I cannot allow that to go unchallenged.

'There is no reason why oil cannot be developed and the penguins and the Falklands way of life safeguarded,' he continues. 'I think the majority of the population would agree with that strategy, but their views are often ignored by people in power. They have their own agenda with vested interests.'

Further ornithological information is available at http://www.seabirds.org/falklands.htm ❏

Michael Griffin

MICHAEL FOLEY

In Dublin's fair city

The surprise banning of a Dublin listings magazine has raised a number of questions, chief among them: why does Ireland still have a Censorship of Publications Board?

The news that Ireland's Censorship of Publications Board was of the opinion that the listings magazine *In Dublin* was 'frequently or occasionally indecent or obscene' was something of a shock to most citizens. But more surprising even than the subsequent ban on the magazine was the revelation that the Board was still in existence.

The present *In Dublin* is very different from its forerunner, a radical magazine with serious editorial content. But it was not the content, nor even the scantily clad babes on its cover, that offended the five members of the Board. It was the ads for 'massage parlours', 'health clubs', sex chat lines and call girls, a fact that was only revealed when Mike Hogan, publisher of *In Dublin*, sought a judicial review of the decision. The High Court lifted the ban on condition that the ads did not reappear; it criticised the manner of the banning but refrained from commenting on the Board.

Hidden from public scrutiny, the CPB has been quietly banning away for years. Publications such as *Butchboys*, *The Best of Asian Babes* and *Stories for Men Who Need it Bad*, largely published abroad, are unambiguously pornographic and for many people are not the stuff of a free speech campaign. But *In Dublin* is part of the Irish mainstream. Mike Hogan publishes other magazines, including the reputable current affairs magazine, *Magill*, whose editor, Emily O'Reilly, resigned after newspapers implied that *In Dublin* had been more than complicit and aware of where the adverts were coming from.

The Board has a sorry history: it was created in 1929 on the recommendation of the Committee on Evil Literature and was problematic from the start. Nowhere was there a clear definition of what it was to ban. The long title of the establishing act actually refers to 'unwholesome' literature and, for the next 30 years or so, in the name of banning the 'unwholesome', the Board banned some of the most important works of the 20th century to keep 'evil' influences out of Ireland. Many of those influences were, of course, Irish. It banned James Joyce's *Stephen Hero* but not *Ulysses*; Samuel Beckett, Walter Macken, Sean O'Faolain, Edna O'Brien and Kate O'Brien all fell foul of its strictures, as did Brendan Behan and many more. Possibly the last major work of literature to be banned was John McGahern's *The Dark* in 1965. Madonna's *Sex*, a book of explicit photographs of the singer, was the last great *cause célèbre*; it was banned in 1992, but not before 2,500 copies had been sold between its importation and the Board's announcement of the ban.

The Board is an outdated body with no place in modern Ireland. However ridiculous, its job is to protect the public from being depraved by seeing, or reading, something obscene; ads couched in euphemistic and titillatory fashion of themselves do not deprave. The more significant question is whether the services advertised were illegal and if the publisher knew what he was advertising. If the answer is yes, then the publisher should have been prosecuted rather than the magazine banned. That is why we have a rule of law and public courts; it is how things are done in democracies.

The government has since announced an inquiry into censorship and pornography, on the Internet as well as in magazines and films. Whether justice minister John O'Donoghue plans to repeal Ireland's antiquated censorship laws or extend them to take into account new technology, remains a matter of speculation. ❏

Michael Foley is a lecturer in journalism at the Dublin Institute of Technology and a media commentator with the Irish Times

ALEJANDRA MATUS

Digging up the dirty war

Chile's establishment would rather forget the past; journalists who choose to remember can find themselves on the run

On 14 April 1999 Judge Rafael Huerta of the Santiago High Court ordered police to go to the premises of Planeta publishers and seize 1,000 copies of the first edition of my book *The Black Book of Chilean Justice*. In the afternoon they raided other bookshops and took away the remainder. More than six years of research, interviews and writing ended up in a police cellar within 24 hours of the launch.

While Planeta's general manager Bartolo Ortiz, accompanied the police to his depository, editor Carlos Orellana called me to break the news. My partner and I had arrived from Miami a few days before the launch and wanted to stay one week more to visit relatives we had not seen for a year. My immediate reaction was to contact the press. News crews were on their way when my brother Jean-Pierre, a lawyer, rang. A warrant was imminent and, though I could be freed on bail after a few days in jail, the judge would probably issue an order preventing me from leaving Chile until the trial was over. 'You've got to leave the country immediately,' my brother urged. I considered staying to face the music, but the publisher persuaded me to leave. We bought the first available tickets to Buenos Aires.

We learned later that the seizure had been ordered by Judge Servado Jordan, president of the High Court from 1996 to 1997 and one of the personalities in my book. Under the Domestic Security Law, any publication or broadcast that 'offends' the president, his ministers, generals and judges can be deemed a crime against national security and its author liable to up to five years in prison. Since it was approved in

1990, the law has been applied to 17 journalists, four of them in cases related to Judge Servado Jordan. As a result, freedom of expression 'is more violated in Chile than in any other country of the West', according to a report issued by Human Rights Watch last year.

We knew the venture was a risky one, but thought that after nine years of democratic revival things wouldn't be too bad. My objective was to describe corruption, nepotism and abuses of power by members of the High Court, but I soon realised that a compilation of specific and anecdotal cases was insufficient response to the deficiencies in the Chilean legal system. Such vices were merely the 'footnotes' to far greater problems.

I could not forget that the judiciary's lack of independence during the Pinochet dictatorship had stripped thousands of people of their legal protection and, ultimately, cost them their lives. Nor could I ignore the ordinary contempt of Chileans towards their own courts, above all by our leaders who, time and again, abandoned the promises of reform that were supposed to make them more democratic. *The Black Book* therefore discusses the High Court's conduct since its inception till the present. I focused chiefly on the military regime, the one that benefited most from the insanity of the judiciary.

I waited 10 days in Buenos Aires before going back to Miami where I now spend my time between computer and telephone, trying to sort things out. Bartolo Ortiz and Carlos Orellana at Planeta spent two and a half days in jail but were absolved of wrongdoing in the Court of Appeals. I have been denounced to Interpol as a 'rebel' and a warrant is out for my arrest. I appealed to the Inter-American Commission of Human Rights and it gave the government 10 days to take due measures to secure my personal safety and right to free expression. Santiago ignored the demand.

Meanwhile, copies of *The Black Book of Chilean Justice* gather dust in a police cellar. ❏

Alejandra Matus is a Chilean journalist based in Miami.

January

1 *The Times,* The *Guardian, Financial Times, International Herald Tribune, Time,* and *Newsweek* go on sale at special kiosks in Moscow and other Soviet cities

5 'Don't Worry, Be Happy', by Bobby McFerrin, tops the German pop charts, chased by 'Bring Me Edelweiß' by Edelweiß

10 Mikhail Gorbachev warns the Soviet Communist Party that it has no right to rule

Political parties in Hungary legalised

4 Muslims in Bradford, Birmingham and other UK cities burn Salman Rushdie's new novel, *The Satanic Verses*

ⓞ **Police in Prague trigger a six-day wave of protests after breaking up a demonstration in Wenceslaus Square to mark the 20th anniversary of the death of Jan Palach, the student who set himself on fire in protest at the Soviet suppression of the 1968 'Prague Spring'. Vaclav Havel, dramatist and co-founder of Charter 77, is among 14 dissidents arrested. In February, he is sentenced to nine months for 'hooliganism'**

ⓞ Britain's Thames TV is cleared of charges that it had prejudiced an official inquest into the SAS killing of three IRA suspects in Gibraltar in the documentary *Death on the Rock*

ⓞ **Father Stanislaw Suchowolec, a colleague of Father Jerzy Popieluszko, the pro-Solidarity priest murdered in 1984, is found asphyxiated in his smoke-filled flat in Bialystok, northeast Poland**

February

FW de Klerk succeeds PW Botha as leader of South Africa's National Party and pledges to end apartheid

Newspaper magnate Rupert Murdoch launches Britain's first satellite TV service, Sky

11 Traditionalists objecting to the consecration of Barbara Harris as the first woman bishop in Anglican history are booed by an 8,000-strong congregation in Boston

14 February Ayatollah Khomeini calls on all Muslims to seek out and execute Salman Rushdie, author of *The Satanic Verses*, and all others involved in its publication

15 **The last Soviet soldier leaves Afghanistan**

Man of Iron, **Andrez Wajda's film about the Gdansk shipyard strike and the birth of Solidarity, completed in 1987, gets its première in Warsaw**

March

7 China imposes martial law in Tibet

East German authorities refuse to distribute a German-language edition of the Soviet weekly *Neue Zeit* because it contains an interview with Solidarity leader Lech Walesa

24 The tanker *Exxon Valdez* runs aground in Prince William Sound, Alaska

26 **Soviet Union holds multi-candidate elections for the Congress of People's Deputies. Moscow mayor Boris Yeltsin wins a large majority**

29 **Hungary's Communist Party approves a law allowing 'anyone, including private individuals, to found a paper, local or commercial radio or television station'**

April

5 Vietnam announces it will withdraw its troops from Cambodia

8 At the 62nd Academy Awards ceremony, Oliver Stone is awarded an Oscar for best directe for *Born on the Fourth of July*. *Cinema Paradiso* wins Best Foreign Language Film, and 'Under th Sea', from *The Little Mermaid*, wins Best Original Song

A thousand Nigerian police descend on Asero stadium, Abeokuta, in 'Operation Silenc Fela' on the occasion of Fela Kuti's first concert since leaving jail

14 The prime minister and president of Georgia resign after 19 demonstrators ar shot in Tbilisi

17 Solidarity is registered as a legal organisation

20 Czechoslovakia's first multi-party elections since 1946

27 *Bay Watch* hunk David Hasselhoff's 'Looking for Freedom' races to the top of the Germa pop charts

May

5 Prime Minister Margaret Thatcher celebrates her 10th year in power

Vladimir Kryuchkev tells *Izvestiya* that the KGB will henceforth report to th public on its major operations

16 Mikhail Gorbachev shakes hands with Deng Xiaoping, marking the end of 30 years o tension between the communist powers. A few hundred metres away in Tiananmen Square i occupied by half a million pro-democracy demonstrators and 3,000 students on hunger strike Four days later, martial law declared in Beijing

17 *Moscow News* publishes an article suggesting that the NKVD, forerunner of th KGB, may have been responsible for the massacre of over 5,000 Polish officers in th Katyn Forest, Smolensk, in 1940

25 Gorbachev is elected president of the Soviet Union

Hungary grants workers the right to strike for the first time in the country' post-war history

Some 300–400,000 members of the Turkish-speaking minority are 'encouraged t leave' Bulgaria following the 'change-of-name' campaign launched in autumn 1985 Analysts say the move is aimed at camouflaging the economic collapse that ha occurred under President Todor Zhivkov, but it only exacerbates it. Bulgarian spend the summer milking the cows, collecting the eggs and cutting the harvests th Turks were forced to abandon

June

1 Amnesty reports that more than 5,000 Palestinians have been held in administrative detentio without charge or trial since the beginning of the *Intifada*

4 Chinese People's Liberation Army open fire on pro-democracy protesters in Tiananme Square in the early hours, killing over 2,000 people and wounding thousands more

Solidarity wins 99 of the 100 seats in the new Polish senate

6 Wild with grief, mourners tear at the shroud of the Ayatollah Khomeini as his bier is carrie to a burial site south of Tehran

1989

12 President Gorbachev and Chancellor Kohl of West Germany sign Bonn Document, affirming right of states to determine their own political systems
15 President Slobodan Milosevic promises to protect a crowd of one million Serbs near Pristina from alleged Kosovar Albanian aggression. At a rally to commemorate the 600th anniversary of the Battle of Kosovo, he says: 'Nobody will beat you again'
21 The siege of Jalalabad ends with a crushing defeat for the Afghan *mujahedin*
28 The first three chapters of Alexander Solzhenitsyn's *Gulag Archipelago* are published in the Estonian monthly, *Looming. Darkness at Noon*, by Arthur Koestler, is finally published in Hungary

July

5 Former South African president PW Botha visits Nelson Mandela in prison
14 Bicentenary of the French Revolution celebrated in Paris
17 **Poland restores diplomatic relations with the Vatican**
Former President Reagan's National Security Advisor Rear Admiral John Poindexter, tells Congress he authorised the diversion of money from arms sales to Iran to the Contra rebels in Nicaragua
31 **Soviet newspapers announce the publication of accurate maps of Moscow for the first time in 50 years. The censorship board announces it has lifted all restrictions on the work of banned authors, except those calling for the overthrow of the state**

August

8 The Contras disband, ending the war with Nicaragua's Sandanistas
14 **The West German embassy in Budapest closes because of overcrowding by would-be asylum seekers**
24 **Poland becomes the first Soviet bloc country to elect a non-communist prime minister**
29 **There are strikes in Moldova, riots in Uzbekistan and fighting in southern USSR**

September

5 President Bush commits US$7.86 billion to an anti-drug war, both in Latin America and on the streets of America. 'Our most serious problem today,' he says, 'is cocaine and, in particular, crack'
11 **Hungary opens its borders with Austria, allowing 60,000 East Germans, posing as holiday-makers, to cross into the Federal Republic. East German media accuse Bonn of provocation and call Budapest 'a Judas' for 'accepting pieces of silver' in exchange for lifting its borders**

Above, T-shirt in Moscow – Credit: Rex

Right, Prague 1989: strikers fill Wenceslaus Square – Credit: Ian Berry/Magnum

October

1 **Seven thousand East Germans arrive in West Germany by train from various destinations**

12 The Pope celebrates a mass in Dili, East Timor, attended by 100,000 people

15 Eight South African nationalists are freed from jail, including Walter Sisulu

17 **The World Psychiatric Association votes to re-admit the USSR on condition that its membership will again be suspended if psychiatric abuse for political reasons is found to be continuing**

18 **Erich Honecker is ousted by his party after 18 years as the East German leader**

19 After 15 years in jail, the 'Guildford Four' are freed when their convictions are judged 'unsafe'

23 **On the 33rd anniversary of the 1956 Hungarian uprising, acting President Matyas Szuros proclaims the birth of a new republic**

28 **Seven hundred people are arrested at a demonstration in Prague to mark the 71st anniversary of Czech independence**

November

1 **East Germans are granted permission to travel to Czechoslovakia without a visa. 4 Demonstrators in East Berlin call for press freedom and democratic elections**

7 **Thousands of protestors stage an 'anti-Revolution Day' rally in**

Moscow to rival official celebrations marking the 72nd anniversary of the October Revolution

The entire East German cabinet resigns

9 Communist Party leader Gunter Schabowski says East Germans are free to leave. Thousands clamber over the 103-mile Berlin Wall. 'I am no longer in prison,' shouts one man. The mayor of West Berlin, Walter Momper, says: 'the Germans are the happiest people in the world today.' By 12 November, a million East Germans have visited the West. The USSR praises the event as 'symbolic', but warns Bonn against changing its borders

10 Todor Zhivkov, Bulgarian head of state for 35 years, is dropped from the politburo

17 TV viewers observe that news bulletins, which previously dismissed protests as illegal assemblies, now screen full accounts. On 25 November, TV and radio provide live coverage of Prague Spring leader Alexander Dubcek's speech in Wenceslaus Square, delivered to the largest crowd in Czech history. Dubcek has been lost in obscurity for 20 years. 'Once already we have been in the light, ' he says, 'and we want it again.' The next day, the government resigns

18 Bulgarians demand free election in the biggest protest rally for 20 years

22 The Brandenburg Gate reopens

24 **East German Politburo resigns**
27 **Czechoslovakia basks in the first labour strike since 1946**
   Soviet parliament passes a law allowing Estonia, Latvia and Lithuania to run own economic affairs within the USSR's federal structure
30 Phil Collins' 'Another Day in Paradise' tops the German chart

December

3 **Despite tempestuous seas, Gorbachev flies from meeting Pope John Paul II to a summit with George Bush on a ship near Malta. Soviet spokesman Gennady Gerasimov tells the press that the Cold War ended 12.45pm (11.45 GMT)**
   The Nobel Peace Prize is awarded to the Dalai Lama
14 Augusto Pinochet is ousted by elections after 16 years in power
   Andrei Sakharov, Nobel-winning nuclear physicist and dissident, dies at home
20 US troops sweep through Panama City, mopping up resistance and continuing the hunt for former president Manuel Noriega, wanted in the US on drug charges
22 Dramatist Samuel Beckett dies
25 **What begins as a small protest on 16 December in the mining town of Timisoara erupts into a 10-day civil war culminating on Christmas Day**

Above, Romanian revolutionaries outside the captured Communist HQ – Credit: Leonard Freed/Magnum

Right, Dubcek returns to Prague – Credit: Ian Berry/Magnum

ith the execution of Romanian dictator, Nicolae Ceaucescu and his wife near his urning palace in Bucharest. A mass grave is subsequently discovered in Timisoara, ontaining 4,630 bodies

Э Vaclav Havel takes up post as Czechoslovakia's new president, appointing US usician Frank Zappa as a special adviser on cultural relations with the West ❏

Compiled by **Brydie Bethall, Saul Lipetz, Catherine Jackson, Margaret Ng, Syra Morley, Natasha Schmidt**

After the fall

**The year is 1989.
A wave of revolution, unexpected and
uncontrolled, is gathering momentum
on the fringes of the USSR.
Within a year or two, it will have swept
away the entire Soviet Empire and
brought the Cold War to an end**

Cold Peace

In the absence of peace, your plain man's mind might think
there will be war. There being no war,
it seems to your learned mind
that this is peace. But it is and will be neither.

György Petri

GUNTER GRASS

1989

Driving back to Lauenburg from Berlin, we tuned in as usual to the
Third Programme, so we got the news late, but when it finally
came I cried out in joy and in panic like thousands of others I'm sure:
'Madness! Sheer madness!' and then – like Ute, who was at the wheel –
sank into thoughts running both forward and back. Meanwhile, an
acquaintance who lived on the other side of the wall and worked in the
archives of the Academy of Arts, keeping watch then as now over literary
estates, was likewise late in receiving the glad tidings, which reached him
like a time-bomb.

The way he tells it, he was jogging home from the Friedrichshain –
nothing out of the ordinary, because even East Berliners had taken up
that American-inspired form of self-castigation by then – when at the
intersection of the Kathe-Niederkirchnerstrasse and Botzowstrasse he
came upon an acquaintance who was likewise panting and sweating from
his jog. Bobbing up and down, they agreed to meet for a beer that
evening, and that evening he repaired to the acquaintance's spacious flat,
where, since his acquaintance was employed in what the East called
'material production', my acquaintance was not particularly surprised to
find a newly laid parquet living-room floor, an achievement utterly
beyond the means of an archival paper-pusher in charge of nothing more
than footnotes.

They had a Pilsner, then another and, before long, a bottle of
Nordhauser schnapps appeared on the table. They talked about the old
days and their children and the ideological constraints at parent-teacher
meetings. My acquaintance – who comes from the Ore mountains, on
whose slopes I had sketched dead trees the year before – told his
acquaintance he was planning a ski trip there that winter with his wife
but was having trouble with his Wartburg – the tyres, both front and
back, had hardly any tread left – and hoped his acquaintance could put

him on the track of some snow tyres: anyone who could have a parquet floor laid by a private person under the conditions of 'actually existing socialism', as the regime was called at the time, would have an idea of how to get hold of so precious a commodity.

As we arrived home in Behlendorf with the good news from the radio now in our hearts, the volume on the television set in the living room of my acquaintance's acquaintance was turned down low so the two of them could go on undisturbed about the tyre problem, and the man with the parquet floor said the only way to get snow tyres was to come up with some 'real money' but he could find him some carburettor jets. Glancing over at the silent screen, my acquaintance

thought the programme must be a feature film of some kind because it showed young people climbing the Wall and sitting astride it while the border police stood idly by. When my acquaintance's acquaintance was made aware of the flagrant disregard for the Wall's protective function, he muttered: 'Typical,' and the two men quickly dismissed the tastelessness of 'yet another Cold War product' so as to get back to the subject in hand – the bald, regular and unavailable snow tyres. The subject of the archives and the papers of the more or less important writers housed there never came up.

As we switched on the TV set, deep in thought by then over the coming post-Wall period, my acquaintance's acquaintance had not yet decided to take the few steps over the newly laid parquet floor to turn up the volume, but when he finally did there was not another word about tyres: it was a problem the new period and its 'real money' could solve instantly. Stopping only to down the rest of the schnapps, they made their way to Invalidenstrasse, which was jammed with cars, more Trabants than the relatively expensive Wartburgs, trying to cross the – wonders of wonders – open border. And if you listened carefully, you could hear everyone, well, nearly everyone who wanted to cross over to the West on foot or in a Trabi, you could hear then all either shouting or whispering 'Madness!' just as I had shouted 'Madness!' outside Behlendorf before sinking into my reverie.

I forgot to ask my acquaintance how, when and for which currency he finally managed to come by his snow tyres. I never found out whether he and his wife, who'd been an ice-skating champion during the days of the German Democratic Republic, ever got to celebrate the New Year in their Ore mountain retreat. Life just kept moving on.❏

Günter Grass's latest book, My Century, *will be published by Faber and Faber in November*
This extract was translated by Michael Henry Heim

PATRICK SMITH

Dark victory

US post-Cold War triumphalism masks a manifest uncertainty about its destiny in the 21st century

In late April 1945, on one of the final days of WWII, a poignant scene unfolded on the banks of the River Elbe some miles southwest of Berlin. US troops moving eastward met Soviet troops whose advance had begun in Stalingrad. When the two armies met, a spontaneous excitement erupted. Amid the last dead of the war came relief and hope – a glimpse, these soldiers thought, of a different future. 'You get a feeling of exuberance,' a US correspondent wrote that day, 'of a great new world opening up.'

It never did. The brief dream of a world order in which differences were recognised, respected and then transcended was shared by many millions. But it gave way by 1947 to the nightmare decades of the Cold War – those 42 years during which the matter of difference froze the world in a grotesque state of hostility and division.

The Cold War was not inevitable: it was the intended consequence of political judgments that began even before the Third Reich collapsed. We know this now, even if we have not yet accustomed ourselves to the implications of this fact of history. And we know that the most fundamental of these judgments were made not in Moscow, as we long supposed, but in Washington.

This assertion would have been heresy only a few short years ago. But the notion that the USA was the prime mover in shaping the Cold War world is not so difficult to grasp. For one thing, scholars are beginning to revise all that never-quite-credible Cold War history. An important example is Carolyn Eisenberg's 1996 work, *Drawing the Line: The American Decision to Divide Germany*, from which I have drawn the above account of that spring day long ago on the Elbe.

For another, the US response to the Cold War's end is very like its reaction to the Allied victory in 1945. The 1990s resemble the 1950s in this important respect: as the USA divided the world then, so it seeks to divide it again now. As the peace of 1945 rapidly evolved into half a century of reckless East-West tension, so has the 'peace dividend' promised when Germans dismantled their Wall in 1989 eluded us ever since.

To cast this comparison more generally, now as in the 1950s, Americans can be fairly described as lost in their own sense of triumph. Now as then, we – we Americans – look out upon the world and consider it somehow ours to be remade in our own image.

Triumphalism: the charge is familiar enough. What is the substance of it? What are its consequences?

At this point, it is refracted throughout US politics, culture and attitudes. Subtly or otherwise, it is evident in everything from movies and advertising to humour, eating habits, athletic competitions, stock market strategies, trade policy – it would be difficult to complete the list. It is the new US ethos; its dimensions are psychological as well as political – individual as well as national. To borrow a phrase from the US writer Tom Engelhardt, triumphalism is our updated, post-Cold War version of the 'victory culture' that arose in the aftermath of WWII.

Its most important manifestations are several. In the name of our triumph, Americans have closed down their public discourse, or – better, perhaps – prevented it from opening up at a moment when it is urgent that it should. This is producing an alarming corrosion of America's political life. Urgent questions go undebated. A widespread complacency – both in and out of government – threatens the institutions of democracy by encouraging Americans to assume that their common inheritance is eternal, requires no vigilance, and can withstand any abuse.

In turn, this has produced a dedication to globalism that borders on religious belief. We may define globalism as the spread of neo-liberal economic principles around the world: deregulation, the wholesale privatisation of public institutions, an unshakable faith in the primacy of unfettered markets. But let us understand the term as it is actually meant. As even its most convinced advocates acknowledge, globalisation amounts to Americanisation. And in this it is not terribly new: it is merely a restatement of the West's Cold War notion of human progress: to modernise means to westernise; to advance you must emulate us. To

modernise means to Americanise, we say now. We have even attached a
certain finality to this proposition: history has ended; the Hegelian
process has run its course, and its end result is the US model.

So have Americans again divided the world – in the name of making
it one. We distinguish today between those who conform to the
principles of Anglo-American neo-liberalism and those who do not –
those who submit and those who hesitate or refuse. At the one extreme,
there are the 'rogue states', nations demonised for their outright denial
of US supremacy. At the other there is Britain, a logical ally as the
birthplace of the principles of free exchange, the logic of the
marketplace. In between, one finds the vast majority: nations eager to
participate in the global economy but unwilling to sacrifice all social
coherence – all sense of community, identity and belonging – to the
effort.

There is in America's post-Cold War thinking an immense,
potentially fatal flaw. It has to do not only with what Americans assert
about themselves and the rest of the world, but with what they miss in
the course of making their shrill assertions. The problem is immense
because it involves America's place in the global order; potentially fatal in
that, left unattended, it could well inflict fundamental damage upon US
relations with the rest of the world in the coming century.

Americans today suffer a kind of narcissism, a failure of vision. As we
did after WWII, we have chosen not to see others as they are, or to see
ourselves as we are – or finally to see ourselves among others. This is the
true meaning of US triumphalism. Wherever we look, we see only
reflections of ourselves.

Narcissus was not an unhappy god – though he met a tragic end.
While he lived he was content enough to contemplate his own visage.
But as the wise Greeks understood, his was a superficial beauty, for there
is nothing attractive about self-absorption. And as the myth implies in
every version that comes down to us, Narcissus had two problems: not
only did he see himself reflected everywhere, he blotted from his vision
all else.

This is America's most fundamental failing in the post-Cold War era.
As a nation, we do not see the rest of the world as it is. To a greater or
lesser degree, the problem has been the same for the 100 years that have
passed since the USA, with its invasion of the Philippines, effectively
chose empire over democracy. It is a problem of leadership, of the view

PATRICK SMITH

of the world our institutions – political, cultural, social, economic – encourage us to cultivate.

Everyone knows the world is changing. But the neo-liberal version of the process we all witness is wholly inadequate – a distorted picture. The irony here is simple: it is the USA that is stuck in the past, even as it proclaims itself herald of the planet's future.

What would Americans see if they could see straight? The question is as important now as it was in the early postwar era. Now as then, the world seeks to redefine itself. It is not, certainly, awaiting new instructions from the United States. Rather, in one nation after another one finds people endeavouring to become themselves again – that is, to define themselves according to their own pasts and aspirations, as opposed to a global conflict not of their making, in which the frames of reference – East-West, left-right, for-against – were not their own.

'Become who you are!' Nietzsche once admonished. It is as if humanity is finally undertaking the realisation of this extraordinarily insightful piece of advice. History did not end when the Berlin Wall fell: on the contrary, it began again. And among the remarkable aspects of this phenomenon is how, in one nation after another, it has picked up precisely where it stopped, frozen in time, at the Cold War's onset in the late-1940s.

There is evidence of this impulse on every continent. It can be seen in Germany, in South Africa, in Iran, in numerous Latin American nations, in Japan, in Indonesia. The project is different in each case – this could hardly be otherwise – but we can call it by a single name. We can call it reinvention. It reaches far beyond the question of post-Cold War identity. It also involves a revaluation of the very ideals that were so long presumed to emanate from the West: democracy, self-determination, progress and so on. This is salutary – a turn of potentially great moment. It means that the human community again proposes to live not by obliterating difference – an impossible task – but by acknowledging difference precisely to transcend it.

It is disheartening to recognise how at odds Americans are with this undertaking, this collective recovery process. Certain leaders embody this thinking: Havel in the Czech Republic, Mandela in South Africa, Khatami in Iran (p10). There are others. They are, fair to say, the Nehrus, Nassers, Nkrumahs and Arbenzes of their time. But does the USA understand them? Even when these figures have managed friendly relations with Washington, that is doubtful. The next question is what the United States will do as this new generation of leaders begins to realise its vision. Consider how many of those of that earlier era were subverted because they did not conform.

It is highly debatable whether the USA won the Cold War. It borders on hubris for Americans to suppose that they were primarily responsible for the Soviet collapse. 'Any suggestion that any United States administration has the power to influence decisively the course of a tremendous domestic political upheaval in another great country is simply childish.' That is George Kennan, the architect of Cold War containment, writing in 1992. Kennan, who was hardly soft on the Soviets, went on to assert that the Reagan and Bush administrations, which claimed that their hard line toward Moscow ended the Cold War, prolonged it by encouraging conservatives in the Kremlin: 'The general effect of Cold War extremism was to delay rather than hasten the great change that overtook the Soviet Union.'

What does Kennan bring to the argument? The core notion should be clear: it has to do with human agency, the inner dynamics of a society as the primary source of change. The US ignored this during the Cold War and ignores it today. But to acknowledge the internal dynamics of other societies is an act large in its import: it is to acknowledge the autonomy of others. And to recognise that as an attribute of the post-Cold War era is to understand that US power has passed its zenith. Boutros Boutros Ghali, the former secretary-general of the United Nations, made this point succinctly in his recent book, *Unvanquished*. 'Single-superpower hegemony is a transitory phenomenon,' he wrote.

To resist this truth is a regrettable impulse, of course, but it is also understandable. Facing the new reality requires a fundamental alteration of America's idea of itself – an idea that has prevailed for more than a century and one shared by many others, it must be said. But the inevitable decline of US power – relatively and absolutely – raises questions Americans cannot avoid forever: can the US live in an undivided world? Can it live without an enemy?

These are not new questions. But they are frighteningly relevant – frightening because one now suspects more strongly than ever that the answer is: 'No, not as Americans now think of themselves.' And no nation has ever changed its idea of itself easily, or without great upheaval.

There is one saving grace to be found in America's current thinking.

It is difficult to discern, but it is there beneath the surface of all that Americans say and do. In all the apparent self-confidence and bluster one detects a deep uncertainty as to our future – and, indeed, even our present circumstances. It is as if the true inner life of the United States now unfolds behind a facade – as if Americans do not quite believe themselves as they trumpet their triumph. It is as if we hear our own voices, and gaze at our own image, with a deep suspicion that our time, our 'American century,' is drawing to a close.

And in that suspicion is our ray of hope. ❑

Patrick Smith *was, for many years, a correspondent based abroad writing mainly for the* International Herald Tribune. *His most recent book is* Japan: A Reinterpretation *(Pantheon/Vintage, 1997/1998)*

Something Unknown

Towards that something unknown
we'll come up against,
do we strive or are we driven?
the blue flower
of a new world, of new love,
enticing us, keeps flickering on and off:
will it lure us into a swamp?

How can you tell.
'Let it all be different now' –
the impulse, desire for that is no more than just:
so run-to-ground we were,
so pissed off we are!
As for self-pity , you can't object to that:
who else, ever at all, felt sorry for us?
And anyway,
we should ourselves
know best – if anyone does –
why we deserve
pity.

All the same, what lies ahead?
What lies ahead? I say.
It's the question
you can't evade
and can't answer.

As for the clot, it is
slowly, yes,
and also surely
swimming
towards the heart. ❑

György Petri is an Hungarian poet. The poems on this page and on p37 are from Eternal Monday, a collection of his poetry published by Bloodaxe Books in September this year
Translated by George Gömöri and Clive Wilmer

IRENA MARYNIAK

In God we trust

**While Boris Yeltsin played politics in Moscow, the Muslims of
his southern provinces were mounting a more serious challenge**

A few weeks after taking hundreds of hostages from a Russian hospital
in June 1995, Shamil Basayev, the Chechen warlord behind the
recent Islamist rebellion in Dagestan, gave an interview in which he
railed not at Russia's politicians or military, but against its national
emblem: the two-headed eagle. It was a monstrous symbol, he said,
contrary to God's design. If a freak like that were ever born, any right-
minded person would kill it. There are plenty of perfectly healthy
symbols on offer: the Chechen wolf, for example, even the bear. 'Until
the Russian nation finds another image by which to recognise itself,'
Basayev declared, 'it will never be spiritually or morally sound.'

Emblems tell of identity and community. Like tribal totems, the
pioneer anthropologist Emile Durkheim once wrote, they objectify the
forces which form, protect and threaten us. Ceremony and ritual, with
their symbolism secular or sacred, are an affirmation of group aspiration
and the urge to create a cohesive and safe human environment. The
totemic symbol expresses a deity, but it is also the flag, the distinguishing
mark of the group: because, Durkheim believed, a god and a society are
the same thing.

Religious loyalties, like tribal ones, offer welcome distinctions in
times when familiar cultural and geopolitical outlines shift or fade. The
reawakening of fundamentalism, nationalism and xenophobia that has
followed the Soviet Empire's dissolution speaks of shattered ideology and
self-perception, and probably still reflects a hazy nostalgia for the
intellectual, emotional and social framework communism once offered.
Religious and national allegiance can give an illusion of community,
where bondage has been fractured. And communality – 'salvation *in*

community' – is, theologically, what the majority religion of eastern and southern Europe, Orthodox Christianity, proffers to the faithful. It is also a tenet and a tradition central to the teaching of the region's other most influential religion: Islam.

The Orthodox legacy, historically, has been a symbiotic interdependence between Church and State. Coexistence with secular powers, provided it doesn't interfere with dogma, is thought less spiritually damaging than becoming an earthly power complete with

army, treasury and diplomatic service, like the Vatican. This was vividly expressed in the Russian Church hierarchy's collaboration with an often aggressively atheist Soviet regime, Stalinism and the KGB over seven decades in which 200,000 clergy died and another half million were repressed. It was reflected too in Archbishop Makarios' blessing of Greek Cypriot terrorism in the 1950s and the Greek Church's support of that country's military junta. The roots of the relationship lie in pre-Ottoman Byzantium where *symphonia*, divinely inspired harmony, was meant to prevail between the emperor and the Orthodox patriarch. After Constantinople fell to the Turks in the 15th century, Christianity and Islam came to determine cultural and subsequently political identity. And in the 19th century, religion became an integral component of newly constructed nationality and statehood. National Churches proclaimed autonomy, 'autocephaly', vis-à-vis the Patriarchate of Constantinople (Istanbul), which was still subordinate to the Ottoman authorities. To be Greek was to be Greek Orthodox, to be Serb was to be Serb Orthodox, and so on unto every nation. In many parts of the post-communist Orthodox world Church and State are still understood as part of an organic religious and political unit, welded by blood and native soil.

All this turns round the notion of a religious institution that does not aim primarily to transmit moral teaching or ideas or articles of faith, but that sees 'belief' as participation in a shared community that contains and revives the spiritual dimension through its disciplines, traditions and, especially, its liturgy. These are the links with numinous energies, the hot-lines to God. So long as that connection is kept alive all shall be well and all manner of things shall be well. Life presents just a single choice: to key into the numinous network and participate in the transfiguration and 'divinisation' of humanity along with all created matter (*theosis*), or to settle for vacuum. Ethics, dogma, philosophy are secondary; logic, argument, debate – misleading. Because 'salvation', the spiritual merger, happens only through the communal body, the *Ekklisia*. So the Church's survival, under any circumstances and almost at any cost, is paramount.

In the nineteenth century, Russian philosophers developed this notion of collectivity (*sobornost*) in relation to State power, ownership, legal procedure and civil society. Semen Frank, for instance, poetically if unhelpfully defined civil society as 'a kind of molecular social bondedness, inwardly connecting the individual elements into a free, plastically flexible whole'. The view that spiritual communality is central to national culture and socio-political organisation, is as popular today throughout the Russian political spectrum as it is in the Orthodox world as a whole. The problem, from a western liberal perspective, is that it leaves little room for innovation, individual dissent, human rights, or social and political tolerance.

The upshot over the past decade has been a series of explosions of ethnic violence in the Balkans, the Caucasus and southern Russia, and a less conspicuous, though potentially as chilling, confrontation between Orthodox Churches and other religions in the region. Non-Orthodox cannot be part of the spiritual community and they may present a threat to national integrity and cohesion, so Church hierarchs have set themselves the task of preserving unity and the national soul. In spring 1994, comparative investigations into attitudes to minorities in Bulgaria, Romania, Greece and Macedonia showed deep-rooted animosity. Education systems emphasise the traditions of the majority and foster feelings of national and cultural supremacy. In Greece, employment in teaching, as well as the upper echelons of the legal and military professions, is limited to Orthodox Christians. Minorities face legal, judicial and administrative restrictions and often insurmountable obstacles in practising their religious faiths. Proselytism is punishable by imprisonment.

In Russia, a law designed to protect the domestic monopoly of the Orthodox Church was introduced in 1997. Earlier the hierarchy had launched verbal onslaughts on other denominations and cults, and at times appeared to be flirting with neo-Nazi and 'red-brown' political groups. Over the past three years there have been incidents of violence against non-Orthodox religious activists including whippings by Cossacks of Russian Adventists; beatings, disappearances and murders of priests of the breakaway 'True Orthodox Church'; and expulsions of Muslims from their place of worship. Moscow's main mosque was stormed in 1996, and people at prayer arrested, beaten, then released. Rhetoric from Church spokesmen, though cautious in emphasising the shared perception of Orthodox and Muslims as guardians against individualism and western influences, rapidly descended to stinging observations about Moscow as 'the third Rome, not the second Mecca' when challenged by the prospect of an Islamic cultural centre being built in the capital.

Serbia saw Slobodan Milosevic make his 1989 watershed speech

commemorating 600 years since the defeat in Kosovo Polje with
Patriarch Pavle at his side. The Church continued to support Serbian
expansionism during the Bosnian war and declined to condemn or
acknowledge alleged massacres, while the paramilitary leader 'Arkan'
reportedly remarked that he listened only to orders of the Serbian
patriarch. The subsequent shift in the Church's position, initially in 1997
when it demanded fairer elections, more recently when it called for
inter-ethnic tolerance during the NATO air campaign and then, most
recently, for Milosevic's resignation, reflects a new-found view that the
regime has well and truly failed and, in so doing, betrayed, the Serb
ethnos.

There were predictions from Russian Church circles in the early
1990s that the stand-off between Orthodox Christians and Muslims in
former Yugoslavia would culminate in 'global conflagration' where the
two religions would 'blend in a turmoil of mutual destruction'. Though
less apocalyptic, Boris Yeltsin's 1994 – 96 war with Islamic Chechnya did
cost 50,000 lives, leaving the northern Caucasus ruined and bankrupt.
As the free market has established itself, the economic divide between
Russians and Muslims has grown in some areas. According to a recent
study conducted by the United States Institute of Peace, half the
economically disadvantaged minority groups of the former Soviet Union
are indigenous Muslims living in the Caucasus and Central Asia. The
link between economic factors and outbreaks of ethnopolitical conflict
in the region are hard to ignore. But, equally, until the early 1990s
Checheno-Ingushetia was the only Muslim republic where no mosque
was registered, even though churches existed for the minority Christian
population.

Today Dagestan, lying in the mountainous territory between
Chechnya and the Caspian Sea, 90% Muslim and with an estimated 7%
of the population supporting radical Islam, is the latest Russian hot spot.
The region is a through road between Chechnya and the Islamic world
further south; more important, it provides Russia with a littoral on the
Caspian Sea through which its claims to a share in the vast offshore oil
reserves in those waters can be further asserted. Ethnic Russians have
been leaving as violence towards non-Muslims grows and kidnappings
become more common. In April this year, the moderate chairman of the
Chechen ministry of religious affairs, Abuzar Sumbulatov, known for his
defence of the Russian population and the Christian minority in

Chechnya, was abducted and is presumed dead.

For months Dagestan has been raided by armed Islamist insurgents often referred to by the Russian media as '*Wahhabis*'. (Wahhabism was a nineteenth-century, puritanical reformist movement within *Sunni* Islam. Today, its main adherents are the Saudi ruling family and the majority of their subjects. It is also found in Pakistan and in other Muslim states of the region.) They are said to be mostly Chechen, led by Shamil Basayev and his Jordanian field commander, Hattab. But the '*Wahhabis*', committed since the early 1990s to establishing a single fundamentalist state in the northern Caucasus, are estimated now to have tens of thousands of supporters in Dagestan itself, many of them young, educated and urban. Members of the group also live in close-knit village communities in central areas of the region. When, in December 1997, a group of fighters attacked a Russian military unit in Buinaksk, well into Dagestani territory, many of those subsequently captured proved to be from Kalakhmakha, a known centre of Wahhabism in the republic. On 9 August 1999, after capturing several mountain villages, Islamist militants declared Dagestan an independent republic. As Moscow rallies, following embarrassing initial reports of Russian helicopter gunships firing missiles at the rebels to scant effect, the indications are that the Kremlin's foothold in the Transcaucasus is once again exceedingly shaky.

What effect any new confrontation between the two-headed eagle and the Chechen wolf would have on the 20-million-strong Muslim population of Russia is a crucial question: Islamic religious identification and practice seems to be growing faster even than that of Orthodox Christians. The supranational sense of belonging to the Muslim community of believers (*Umma*) reinforces an already existing sense of alienation. There is a popular myth among Russians that Muslims, Caucasians and *mafiosi* are all links in a single criminal chain. In Moscow, where the Muslim population has risen from 250,000 to 1 million since 1989, 60% admit to racist sentiment and approve city policies of evicting southerners from the capital. One-quarter of the advertisements for apartments to rent say Caucasians need not apply. Dark-skinned people are randomly searched by police, fined in excess of what the law specifies, detained without charge and beaten in custody. In October 1993, before the Chechen war, up to 9,000 people were deported and 67,000 detained; another 10,000 fled the city. A similar clean-up took place in anticipation of Moscow's 850th birthday in September 1997. We could shortly witness another such operation.

In a country which has seen four prime ministers sacked in 18 months, the debate about democratisation and civil society still revolves around the traditional juxtaposition of western and Russian political thought: individualist secular liberalism versus the nineteenth-century Slavophile notion of communality and Russian specificity. Neo-Slavophile discourse is increasingly dominant along with the view that civil society is a Eurocentric idea, a projection of cultural imperialism cum economic hegemony, not a universal value applicable to a globalising world. Even Russia's 'new liberals' – represented by former first deputy prime minister Boris Nemtsov, another likely candidate for the presidency – advocate a strong State, distance from the West and the missionary role of post-communist Russia as a source of ideas that will save the world from collapse. Television shows discuss astrological predictions that the next 1,000 years will be the Russian millennium. Debate on civil society has given way to a preferred vision of Russia as a strong State with a controlled market economy and a 'harmonious' community integrated by national religion.

But if recently televised remarks from the maverick Russian Orthodox Autonomous Church are to be believed, Orthodox Christianity as spiritual practice, rather than as a side-kick of the national emblem, is in crisis. During Easter 1998, only 1% of the Russian population participated in a liturgy, despite the Church's claims that 80% of Russians are Orthodox. In the first flush of post-communist religious enthusiasm in the early 1990s, Orthodox congregations did double; but Muslim ones tripled. So far, the authorities and the Church have dealt with their dread of Islamic militancy by supporting what they call 'the traditional Islam of the region'. That they should continue to do so now, as Russians watch footage of Albanian children taking pickaxes to Serb Orthodox Churches in Kosovo or read that Christian priests in Dagestan may not walk the streets without fear of violent abuse, is a thing devoutly to be wished. ❏

Irena Maryniak

MICHAEL FOLEY

Bashing the bishops

George Orwell said it was not necessary to live in a totalitarian society to be corrupted by one. In Ireland, Catholic oppression was condoned in the name of the battle against godless communism

It is not only those who lived within eastern Europe who might want to celebrate the collapse of communist regimes. Communism was a godsend to the more authoritarian elements in the West, especially in the Catholic Church. Those brought up as Catholics remember the prayers for the conversion of Russia at the end of the mass, the endless tales of repression, especially of Catholic Poland and Croatia. And, of course, repression of ordinary Poles and Croats was bad enough, but all the more serious when it was of priests and especially bishops. We heard little of the *gulag*, but much about churches that were closed and priests unable to say mass. In that narrative, Archbishop Stepinac and Cardinal Wyszynski were heroes.

Eastern Europe – as an example of what might happen if we strayed from the path of respect for those in authority over us – fulfilled an important function in the West. Nowhere was this truer than in Ireland. The endless articles that now appear portraying Ireland as a liberal, swinging place, with Dublin as the new Paris, are not just the result of a booming economy, but of a new liberalism, a less authoritarian political and social culture, and a more open society than the one portrayed by John McGahern or Edna O'Brien.

Ireland was not a totalitarian state. It gained independence in 1922 and has been a democratic country since, the fourth oldest democracy in Europe. It was probably the only Catholic state not to have succumbed to fascism, totalitarianism or military rule at some stage during the twentieth century, a fact that made the ultra-conservative Irish Catholic Church even more vigilant against communism. In Russia there was the Soviet State and the Communist Party; in Ireland, the Irish State and the Catholic Church. Its priests and bishops oversaw a regime as strictly as any commissars. The clergy intervened in matters of State when they believed it necessary and, from the start, the State made little complaint. Tom Garvin, in *1922: the Birth of Irish Democracy*, explains: 'An ingenious, neat and pious way of saving the ratepayers cash was found by the simple device of closing down state-financed and state-run industrial schools and handing the children over to religious orders.' Those of us who attended Catholic schools can remember priests telling us of their selflessness and of how much it would have cost the State to educate us if they had not been willing to shoulder the responsibility.

Ireland was also a highly secretive state where the Church operated as an alternative system within a system. The State consulted the Church which constantly warned of the consequences of deviating from the true path. It influenced the constitution, ensuring it conformed to its teaching. Until recently its special position was enshrined in the constitution and the State papers are full of references to visits to the bishop's palace in Dublin by members of successive governments seeking approval for proposed legislation or government action from the Archbishop of Dublin.

The secret nature of the Irish State was obsessional. In 1962, it amended the Official Secrets Act, the one it had inherited from the British, to make even more secrets. The Irish Act was a direct result of anti-communist hysteria after the Cuban missile crisis; it made everything emanating from government secret unless specifically made public. So all-embracing was this Act that even the menu in the *Oireachtas* (parliament) restaurant was supposedly secret; and so timid the media that there have been only two prosecutions of journalists under this Act. Of course this alliance of the Catholic Church and a secret State led directly to censorship, of both literature and films. Like so much else this has been dramatically relaxed in recent years.

Over the past 10 years, people in the former communist world have been learning the true nature of their regimes. Archives are being opened; people are coming forward with their stories. A similar process has been taking place in Ireland. It was in 1992 that the Catholic Church was first rocked with the revelation that Eamon Casey, Bishop of Galway, had fathered a child – now in his late-teens – by an American woman. Not only was the woman, Annie Murphy, willing to tell all, for the first time the media was willing to report a story inculpating a high-ranking cleric. The story was broken in the *Irish Times*, so unused to publishing a story of this kind it presented it as one dealing with the misappropriation of public funds; the bishop had used diocesan funds to finance the upbringing of his son.

An increasingly confident media started to break other stories. There was corruption in the beef industry, in the banking system, the political system itself; above all, there were stories about the Church.

In May 1998, the Irish government announced it was establishing a commission to examine the abuse of children who were in the care of religious orders or the State, including primary and secondary schools, from at least the 1940s to the present day. The *Taoiseach* (prime minister), Bertie Ahern, said: 'We must start by apologising. On behalf of the State and of all citizens of the State, the government wishes to make a sincere and long overdue apology to the victims of childhood abuse for our collective failure to intervene, to detect their pain, to come to their rescue.' He also promised a whole range of services for dealing with the damage.

This development came after a three-part television documentary, *States of Fear*, on Irish public service television shocked viewers with its stories of Irish children abused in homes and in what were called 'industrial schools', bleak institutions where children who had sinned by committing a crime, or were themselves the result of sin having been born out of wedlock, were housed in the 1940s and 1950s.

States of Fear was an examination not simply of the misery young children were forced to undergo, but of a culture at a given time. It demanded to know how this could have happened. In the days that followed, a former newspaper editor gave one answer when he revealed how newspapers in the 1950s and 1960s had ignored, often under orders from senior churchmen, events taking place in industrial schools and other Church-run institutions.

What shocked the public was not so much the evidence of physical and sexual child abuse by a relatively small number of monks and nuns, but that these children had been placed in the care of the Church by the State; that they were the victims of an ideology as surely as were the

MICHAEL FOLEY

victims of the *gulag* and, like so many of the latter, they had committed
no crime. Equally shocking to many was the Church's attempt at a
cover-up when the stories began to emerge. It was not, it claimed,

accountable to anyone – with the exception, perhaps, of God – and no-one had the right to demand an explanation.

The Catholic Church exercised its power through the control of childhood, education and motherhood. This it did through its dominance in the education system and the hospital service. Its control of the school system made its priests powerful local figures who, as late as the 1980s, opposed any attempt to enlarge the very small number of secular schools. Through the hospital service it controlled fertility and family planning, and influenced the nursing and medical profession. The best-known instance of the Church's interference in politics was probably the Mother and Child Scheme, an experiment in social medicine in the late 1940s that would have provided free medical services and drugs to expectant mothers and babies. The Church objected: this was communism, it said, and mobilised the medical profession to defeat it.

Ten years after the fall of the Wall Ireland is hardly recognisable. The numbers attending Church services has fallen dramatically. A Church finding it difficult to come to terms with the loss of its authority following revelation after revelation is reeling; corruption in the political system is at last being investigated. Homosexuality was decriminalised without a murmur; the people voted in a referendum to allow divorce. Although much of the machinery of secrecy believed necessary to protect authority from scrutiny is still in place, especially the draconian defamation laws, freedom of information legislation is now on the statute books and the pressure is mounting for further moves away from an authoritarian past. Recently, a priest suggested that the Church should look again at how it funds education given the numbers that are not going to weekly mass, the first sign that the Church might actually move out of education.

And the media is willing to expose what it would at one time have kept under wraps. Some of the coverage has been voyeuristic and intrusive, and some seek to curb its zealous exposure of corruption in high places. But without an external enemy to justify control, Ireland is finding it is probably better to live with a flawed press than with a supine one. ❏

Michael Foley *is a lecturer in journalism at the Dublin Institute of Technology. He is a regular contributor to* Index *and the* Irish Times

JUAN GOYTISOLO

Strangers among us

Europe's long-held fear of Islam continues to shape its political attitudes and social identity

The city of Marrakesh has been an essential reference point in my life for 22 years. During this time I have seen it grow and become more modern without losing the beauty of its human aura because of this. Motorised traffic has, to be sure, increased from year to year, but the horse-drawn carts and small wagons of the *almahales* are still to be seen. There are neighbourhoods with luxury villas for the Millionaires International. Yet the *medina* and the marketplace have kept their energy and liveliness. I live in an exclusively Arab neighbourhood, whose rhythms of life I have made my own. I enjoy the quiet on my patio, the distant din of the crowds on the square, the voices of those who extol their goods in my narrow street, the call to prayer of the *muezzin*, the screams of children, the chirping of birds. At my age, when hearing and vision grow weaker, the sense of smell recovers, and I perceive the scent of spices, orange blossoms and cedarwood. None of these are of measurable value, but they are values.

Before I come to speak of Arab culture, and how it is mistakenly perceived from a western perspective, I would like to remain for a while in Marrakesh. The complexity of the *medina* as an urban space is incompatible with logic and predictability. It invites the passer-by to follow paths that can teach mysterious lessons in topography. The irregularity of the façades and their abrupt, unpredictable angles, lend it the seductive aura of a labyrinth. The functionality of a space laid out in right angles is subject to a strict order of hygiene and control – consecutively numbered block by block, house by house, by a power that has a great interest in registering and classifying its residents. The

Arab *medina* has preserved a certain improvised nature, a model of life to which administrative interventions are foreign. The square in Marrakesh is a challenge for the logic of an open, 'renovated' space. It expresses a great respect for people, for individuals as well as for masses. The edges of the street are blurry and changeable. The wares push into them. The vendors stay in the streets, blocking traffic. Craftwork is carried out before everyone's eyes; the pyramid of exploitation is not veiled.

This composition of public space makes the relationship between classes transparent. It is a theatrical arrangement of workshops and bazaars, an alternation between public and private space, that is a standing call to be curious. In European or North American cities I have always sensed, very strongly, my ageing as something outside life. In Marrakesh I stand in constant contact with life. Walter Benjamin, whom I admire, said it takes a great deal of education to lose yourself in a city the way you do in a forest. I have this education at my disposal. My plumbing of Arab language and culture enables me to look at Islam no longer with ethnocentric blinkers, as do the overwhelming majority of Europeans. Those closest geographically to Islam construct their national identity on its denial. With this I have nothing in common.

Since its advance into the Middle East and the Iberian peninsula, Islam has always been the mirror in which Europeans have seen themselves portrayed in a very special way. Islam is an external picture that questions and worries us. Often it is our negative, and the projection of that which we censure in our internal jurisdiction. It is, therefore, a projection screen for abhorrence and envy, but at times also for a romantic, attractive picture of an unattainable ideal. This is obviously not exclusively a Spanish, nor even a European, phenomenon.

The construction of the other, be it of the barbarian or the noble savage, is a universal phenomenon. It varies according to the historical, cultural and social conditions of the society in which it takes place. It is logical that geographical factors such as nearness and distance play a fundamental role. The fact that certain characteristics, norms and mores are different usually develops among neighbours into an unbridgeable contrast in 'essence'.

Between the eighth and 17th centuries, Islam (Arab or Turkish) assumed a central position for the Christian sphere. Qualitatively, it differs from the rest of the non-European civilisations (the Buddhist, the Brahmanic, etc). The Tunisian historian, Hichem Djalit, saw in this the continuation of a distinctive, persistent 'anti-Islamic sensibility at all levels of the European unconscious'. For the Christian world, Islam has played a consciousness-building role in the identity-endowing dialectic of Self and World. Islam was the Other, the 'intimate enemy', too near to appear completely exotic, too obstinate and coherent to tame or trivialise.

Legends, clichés, rhetoric and whole compilations of Islamic pictures were created by the West. These set up an unbridgeable distance between the 'familiar' (which, of course, is bound up with a consciousness of superiority and self-satisfaction) and the 'foreign' (that is perceived with hostility and contempt). The West and Islam, these two abstract constructs, support and mirror each other in this way. They play a dialectical game with their mirror images. Islam is the concave form, the negative of Europe, that which it has rejected, and that which, at the same time, is its temptation.

The Islam that Spanish Christians came to know was not only a military power with which they had to measure themselves in battles and wars. It was also an ideological-religious enemy, and a philosophical and cultural model, whose superiority and influence shaped Spanish Christians for centuries. The bishops and Church authorities complained that the faithful had stopped using Latin and expressed themselves easily and elegantly in Arabic. Later, this cultural mixing manifested itself in the creation of new, highly original literary and artistic forms, the *Mudejar* style. From the translators school in Toledo, Arab science and philosophy, as well as the philosophy preserved from Greece, spread throughout a Europe that had been cut off from its Graeco-Roman roots by the invasion of the barbarians. The defenders of theses advocated by Avicenna were confronted by Thomas Aquinas during the theological debates at the University of Paris in the middle of the 13th century. Thomas, in turn, supported positions derived from Averroes; and so christianised, unintentionally, an Islamic theological debate. And since Asín Palacios we also know that Dante made use of an Arabic text, translated into Latin and Provençal, on the *miarax*, or 'the nocturnal journey of the Prophet to heaven and hell', in writing the *Divine Comedy*.

This influence, and the tacit processing of Islamic customs, knowledge and cultural models, had consequences. The Spaniards adopted as their own the concept of tolerance, the idea of the crusade, the order of knights, the rosary and the religious lay brotherhoods during Holy Week. The need for defence was accompanied by the wish to disparage a feared and admired opponent. A propagandistic literature arose that drew a distorted and grotesque picture of Muslims. For hundreds of years they were regarded as followers of an imaginary trinity, a false reply to the Christian. Their prophet was represented as a god, a charlatan and a swindler. Their paradise was a bordello. Empirical reality, direct observation and confrontation with facts didn't count. A way of looking at things divorced from reality, which preceded the anti-Islamic discourse, replaced every attempt to acquire knowledge. This written corpus spanned several centuries and disciplines, and in this way gained a terrible power. Imagination veiled and darkened reality. Raimundus Lullus and others with open minds tried to begin a dialogue. Juan de Segovia's efforts aimed at a peaceful meeting and exchange of ideas. These attempts were not able to do anything against the powerful arsenal of insulting myths and legends about Islam and Arabs. Europe's defensive withdrawal during the last centuries has long given way to a conquering offensive. This has tended to strengthen the myths and legends even more.

Basically, it suffices to open any history book to convince oneself of the systematic use of a double terminology. In these books, the western sphere of influence is spoken of in a flattering way, the Arab in a derogatory way. The West speaks of 'expansion', 'economic calling' or 'civilising mission'. Muslims are equated with 'invasion', 'avalanche' or with a 'sudden incursion by hordes'. The very same textbook will describe in the greatest detail the cruelty of the Ottoman Sultan, but cover the burning of heretics during the Inquisition, or the red or white terror of our revolutions, with a veil of discretion.

The historical circumstances of the last 40 years, the struggle against western colonialism, the founding of the state of Israel and the subsequent expulsion of the Palestinians, the civil war in Lebanon and the Iranian revolution, have produced a situation of violence, and placed the Islamic world *en bloc* in the dock. It is now portrayed as a geopolitical danger and a cause of significant world crises.

History, and the West's recent past, however, in no way give it a right to be giving others lessons of any kind. The anti-Islamic propagandist ought to remember that Islam never gave rise to a bloody Inquisition, genocide like that against the Indo-Americans, collective fascist extermination or the use of deadly Hiroshima weapons.

Even well-meaning observers often make the same old mistake of clinging to ethnocentric demands in their view of Islam, and of mechanically carrying their own concepts over to a different cultural sphere. One can't equate Shiism, or Wahhabism, or Salafiya Islam with Protestantism. The Islam of marginalised masses, which serves as a source of identity, has nothing in common with our elite *integrismo*. In order to make clear the misuse of ethnocentric generalisations it would suffice to replace the concept of 'Islamic' with 'Christian'. Polish Catholicism, Irish Protestantism, the Maronite community in Lebanon, Swiss Calvinism, Opus Dei, the Quaker and Mormon communities, as well as the Latin American followers of so-called liberation theology, cannot in any way be understood by labelling them 'Christian religion'. Only someone ignorant, or crazy, could confuse a Christian believer with one of Karadzic's Serbian extremists. Yet to see Islam's intellectual and cultural legacy as the presumed basis for terrorism outrages no-one.

Whoever wishes to free Islam and its spiritual message from this amalgam of fantasies and errors should recall a series of events and fundamental ideas that relate to Islam's cultural and religious dimensions, as well as its social and political ones. Islam, the word that came out of the desert, spread like fire in less than a century. It fastened on large communities of varied origin and culture. This view of life rejects, above all, any kind of discrimination with respect to race or language. It does not insist on the existence of a Church or papal authority. In its spheres of influence it tolerates, under certain conditions, the other religions of the Holy Scripture. Islam permits no priesthood to stand between the faithful and God. The simplicity of its doctrine, the belief in one, and only one, God, Allah, and in Mohammed, God's Prophet, brings the historical cycle of prophesy to an end. Islam is open to all classes and races, to all people who orient themselves towards the *qibla*. The practice of the *Arkan addin*, the Pillars of Islam, enable an identification of the masses of the faithful with the faith. This inner coherence constitutes its power, and has enabled its continued expansions over 14th centuries.

Samuel Huntington forecast a confrontation of civilisations as the consequence of the worldwide triumph of the ideology of progress and globalisation at any price. The scenario serves in reality as an alibi for an unjustified enlargement of the military budgets of the great powers. The prophesy is false because the problem is not even posed in this manner. It is not the struggle among different but non-opposing civilisations that requires a final conclusion, but rather, the struggle of all these civilisations against an uncontrolled modernity.

Some radical groups reduce Islam to an ideology and a political weapon for mobilising the masses. These groups have long ago split away from the main trunk of their world-view and falsified it. To rob Islam of its philosophical and cultural dimension, its rich mystical experience, its artistic and literary legacy, means to impoverish it. The majority of Muslim people live under unworthy and unjust conditions. Our judgments concerning these conditions of life should not entice us to confuse purely chance circumstances with the religious and ethical principles that determine the life of these peoples.

Islam is also the Ottoman architecture of Sinan, the slender minaret of the Kutubiy mosque, the variety and tolerance of the open spaces of *Jemaa el Fna*, the passionate words of the Sufi poet Ibn Arabis, the literary creations of Shiism in Iran – an admirable intellectual sensitivity and subtlety – and the formative ideal of Al Andalus. ❑

Juan Goytisolo *is a Spanish novelist and journalist. This excerpt is from 'On the Familiar and the Foreign: Europe and Islam' published in* Augenzeugen der Geschichte/Eye Witness to History *(English and German text, World's Citizens Society, Hanover 1999)*

OLIVIER ROY

Dangerous ground

The USSR's Afghanistan foray exposed its military weakness and accelerated political instability

The war in Afghanistan was not only symptomatic of the decline of the Soviet empire, it hastened its fall. It also gave us an example of the rise of political Islam and its mutation into the conservative fundamentalism represented by the Taliban. But there is one particular feature of this war not found elsewhere: the alliance between Islamic fundamentalism and the USA. This is due in no small part to the ambiguous role played by Pakistan and Saudi Arabia. The anti-communist – but also anti-Iran – alliance forged in Afghanistan did not survive the collapse of the USSR: Islamic militants who fought in this war can today be found in Kashmir as well as in Afghanistan fighting on behalf of Pakistan; and there is a radical fringe, led by the Saudi dissident Osama bin Laden, that has taken to anti-American terrorism.

The Soviet occupation of Afghanistan marked the most southerly advance of Soviet and Russian troops. It elicited a strong emotional reaction in the West and played an important part in Ronald Reagan's demonisation of the USSR. The US congress voted massive aid to the Afghan resistance; it saw the *mujahedin* as the 'freedom fighters' of its new 'roll back policy' designed actively to push back Soviet influence in the region rather than simply containing it as it had been content to do until this point. In 1986 US-supplied anti-aircraft Stinger missiles changed the balance in the war; in February 1988 Mikhael Gorbachev announced the withdrawal of Soviet troops; a year later they were gone.

Its Afghan adventure was a military setback for the USSR – and not only because of the Stingers. As early as 1983 it was clear that serious problems within the Soviet military would prevent it from winning the war: it was demoralised, undisciplined, riddled with corruption; logistics were totally inadequate. Afghanistan exposed the fact that the Soviet

Afghanistan: Russian troops cover their guns prior to withdrawal — Credit: Solomonov/Novosti

Union, particularly its military machine, had run out of steam (this, no doubt, accounts for the army's failure to act at the actual moment of collapse in 1991), and that the Soviet threat had been greatly exaggerated. But no-one drew the relevant conclusions. It took until June 1996 and the Russian army's debacle in Grozny for anyone to admit that the Soviet military machine had collapsed from within long ago. One consequence of this is that the newly independent states in the region, Uzbekistan for instance, do not see Russia as a military threat. Moscow's only military role in the region is as a spoiler: by taking sides in existing conflicts, it has fanned the flames in places like Tajikistan, Nagorno Karabakh, Abkhazia, even Kosovo.

The Soviet retreat of February 1989 was only one stage of a more widespread withdrawal: the independence of the Soviet republics in 1991 vastly enlarged the area of Muslim control to the south of Russia and resulted in a general withdrawal of Russian troops. They have already abandoned Turkmenistan and Uzbekistan and remain only in Tajikistan. Afghanistan today is part of Central Asia; the old boundaries inherited from the Soviet system are frequently contested as ethnic nationalisms rear their heads. Uzbeks and Tajiks, to cite only one instance, are present on both sides of the Afghan-former USSR border. These permeable frontiers work in favour of ethnic solidarity as the Taliban's cross-border recruitment in the Pashtun heartland that straddles Pakistan and Afghanistan demonstrates: common ethnicity is as important as shared ideology. Smuggling, particularly of drugs, is another beneficiary of the vanishing borders. It happens across all the Afghan borders but is particularly active among the Baluch who operate on horseback between Iran, Pakistan and Afghanistan. From buffer state, Afghanistan has become the crossroads at the centre of a turbulent area.

The war in Afghanistan was an example of the rise of an Islamic movement inspired by Egypt's Muslim Brotherhood and Pakistan's *Jama'at* Islami. It spoke the language of revolution and aimed at the establishment of an Islamic State by way of a political party that shared its ideology. In Afghanistan this was typified by Gulbuddin Hekmatyar's *Hezb-i Islami*, the favoured recipient of Pakistan-administered US military aid (p100). With US agreement and the active support of Saudi Arabia and Pakistan, thousands of volunteers from the Muslim world flocked to Afghanistan to fight alongside the *mujahedin*. Financed by

Saudi and with the logistical help of the Brotherhood, Pakistan's *Jama'at* played an important part in putting in place a network of fundamentalist groups operating out of Peshawar.

But the war also exposed the limitations of these Islamic movements in building the Islamic State of their dreams: they were incapable of overcoming their ethnic and tribal differences. The *Hezb-i* remained essentially a Pashtun group Massoud's *Jama'at*, Tajik. Najibullah had always maintained himself in power by playing on these differences and his communist government did not fall immediately the Soviets left. Once Kabul had fallen to Massoud in April 1992, however, the ethnic nature of the internal conflict became all too apparent with the northern coalition of Tajiks, Uzbeks and Hazaras pitted against the Pashtun *Hezb-i Islami*. The rise to power of the Taliban in 1994 and their capture of Kabul in 1996 highlighted the changing nature of the Islamic movement across the Muslim world. The new radicals were ideologically conservative, *Sunni* to a man and therefore passionately opposed to Iran and the *Shia*, close to the *Wah-abi* of Saudi Arabia and with only one object on the political front: the strict application of the sharia and the seclusion of women. At the same time, the Taliban embodied the revenge of the Pashtun, not at all happy to see Kabul in the hands of other ethnic groups. Indeed, one of the lessons of the Afghan war was that, contrary to its claims, fundamentalism was incapable of bridging ethnic divides.

But this shift in modern Islamic movements towards a more archaic form of fundamentalism is not confined to Afghanistan. In fact, the 1990s saw Islamic movements that had operated on a grand scale retreat into more narrowly nationalist frameworks: *Refah* in Turkey, *Hamas* in Palestine, *Hezbollah* in Lebanon or the *Front Islamique de Salut* (FIS) in Algeria for instance. Meanwhile, neither in Afghanistan nor anywhere else, did the Iranian revolution succeed in spreading its influence outside the *Shia* community, in most cases a minority outside Iran. This 'nationalisation' of the wider Islamic movements left the field open for the new, more internationalist, more conservative tendency of the Taliban, who would, in turn, become more radical.

Once the fighters of the 'Islamic legion' who had come to fight in Afghanistan returned home, they joined, or themselves set up, the most radical of the fundamentalist movements of the 1990s: the *Groupes Islamique Armées* (GIA) in Algeria, Islamic *Jihad* in Egypt and the small groups active in Yemen, Somalia and even in France. Those who stayed in Afghanistan joined the Taliban or, in Pakistan, groups like those sent into Kashmir in spring this year. Since the Gulf war of 1991, these groups have taken a violently anti-western – more specifically anti-US – line. Under the auspices of Osama bin Laden they have been implicated in a succession of attacks on US targets from New York's World Trade Centre in February 1993 to the US embassies in Kenya and Tanzania in August 1998. Iran has lost its pre-eminence as the centre of Islamic terrorism to Afghanistan: all the militants involved in the above attacks, like Sheik Omar and Yusuf Ramzi of the WTC attack, have spent time in the latter.

The evolution of the fundamentalist movement goes hand in hand with a similar trend in Pakistan. Throughout the war, Pakistan used the *mujahedin* it was supporting to play the *Sunni* fundamentalist card and implement an aggressive regional policy, not only against India and Iran, but also in Central Asia. A shadowy network of organisations, based in Lahore and made up of militants who had trained in Afghanistan, was used to destabilise Pakistan's neighbours. And, in spring 1998, Pakistan made its possession of a nuclear weapon official.

From the most loyal US ally in the frontline against the Soviet threat, Pakistan became the 'rogue state' of the region. To its nuclear capability, it now added a militant Islamic posture that led it to provoke a crisis in Kashmir, to shelter radical Islamic militants who were particularly active in Central Asia – as in China's Xinjiang – and to give substantial military support to the Taliban's offensives. Even for a long-term ally like the USA, Pakistan's creeping destabilisation of the region was too much. For the first time, in spring 1999, pro-Indian voices in Washington and Beijing defeated the Pakistan lobbies.

But the seemingly endless war in Afghanistan also had a negative impact within Pakistan. The radical fundamentalist forces that had always supported General Zia were becoming increasingly out of control. Drugs, the crisis in the national economy, the imposition of the *sharia* (Islamic law) – sometimes imposed at a local level in Pashtun tribal areas – repeated riots and rampant smuggling weakened the central government whose only response was a relentless pursuit of the same policies.

This Islamic activism, more centred on Pakistan than on Afghanistan, tended to affect regional alliances. August 1998 saw a largely unremarked series of coincidences: the Taliban offensive against northern Afghanistan coincided with the terrorist attacks on the US embassies. In the course of the Taliban capture of Mazar-i Sharif, a dozen Iranian diplomats and others were assassinated. On 27 August, Washington decided to bomb the Islamists' camps in Afghanistan while Iran mobilised its troops on the Afghan frontier against these same Taliban. Iran and the USA found themselves on the same side in the fight against this new form of Islamic fundamentalism.

Other realignments are under way in Central Asia. Uzbekistan, anxious to distance itself from Russia and draw closer to the USA, had never been close to Iran. During a period of particularly intense Islamic activity in the Ferghana valley, Tashkent had been forced to protest to Pakistan: the chief of the Islamic opposition, Taher Yoldashev, is close to the Taliban. In Tajikistan, on the other hand, ethnic solidarity is everything: the Islamic opposition, exiled in Afghanistan, has not linked up with the Taliban, but with Massoud, who has excellent relations with the neo-conservative government in Dushanbe. Tajiks on both sides of the frontier thus get along together; the Russians are supporting Massoud, at one time their most formidable enemy, against the Taliban. Iran, too, favours Massoud.

The USA has, so far, failed to grasp the significance of these realignments. Its relations with the Taliban, exceedingly warm in 1996 have dropped to freezing since the latter's protection of bin Laden, yet all it has done is demand his removal from Afghan territory. However, the decision, in July this year, to impose an economic boycott on the Taliban may mark the beginning of a new phase in US alliances in the region: a rapid distancing from Pakistan and the Taliban in favour of rapprochement with India and, in a year or two, even with Iran. ❏

Olivier Roy *is a researcher at CNRS (French National Centre for Scientific Research) and the author of* Islam and resistance in Afghanistan *(Cambridge University Press, 1990).* The new Central Asia, or the manufacturing of nations *will be published by I B Tauris (London) later this year*
Translated by Judith Vidal-Hall

SALIL TRIPATHI

Indian angst

The defeat of Congress in 1989 changed Indian politics, society and economics forever

It had been weeks of gruelling election campaigning for many of us. On a winter night in 1989, as pundits on television tried to create soundbites to capture the changed mood of an angry nation, we saw Rajiv Gandhi for the last time as prime minister. He made a dignified farewell address, trying to redeem some of the lost honour.

In 1984, his Congress Party had secured the largest electoral majority in Indian parliamentary elections; in 1989, it had lost more than half the seats, squandering public goodwill spectacularly, losing to a hastily put together coalition, divided against itself but united in its desire to oust Gandhi. The coalition was supported by the extreme left and the extreme right. A weakened centre could not hold. Would things fall apart?

None of us could have foreseen in that exhilarating moment – and change of government through peaceful means in India is exhilarating precisely because it happens so rarely in other developing countries – that Indian politics was undergoing a remarkable shift. With hindsight, after 10 years, it seems crystal clear and inevitable that the nature of Indian politics had changed that night. And not just politics: its economics, and in some respects the society itself, changed.

In pre-1989 India, businesses did little managing; the government's bureaucrats did that with their sub-rules and clauses. One domestic airline ruled the skies, telephones were black and rotary-dial and cellular phones were deemed toys for the rich that India didn't need, because millions didn't have access to drinking water. In that India, Hindu nationalist politicians were seen as whimsical aberrations; Coca-Cola was not available; and the star in the sky was not a Murdoch-owned TV channel. The State-owned broadcaster, *Doordarshan*, had only just begun to make its first soap operas. What enthralled millions of viewers were two shows, *Ramayana* and *Mahabharata*, retelling, with Bollywood kitsch, two of the best-known Hindu epics.

In 1999, everything has changed. It is cool to be rich, to be seen to be wealthy, to be contemptuous of minorities, to suffer from wounded pride as a civilisation. India is a country, not a market, said the 1996 election slogan of the Hindu nationalist Bharatiya Janata Party. It is a new India where the son of a minor politician can whip out an unlicensed gun and shoot a glamourous model who refuses to serve him at an illegal bar after official hours, as happened in Delhi earlier this year. It is an India with more confidence and more assertion, but greater doubts about the 1947 model of a secular, liberal, socialist, democratic republic.

To understand that change, let us go back to 1984, the year Gandhi was swept to power on the strength of a massive sympathy vote following the assassination of his predecessor (and mother) Indira Gandhi by two of her own bodyguards. The shameful rioting after the assassination, which killed thousands of Sikhs, did not stop the Congress juggernaut from winning over 400 of the 547 seats in the parliament.

This was at least partly because Gandhi was supposed to represent India's Camelot era – he would change the way India functioned, with his youthful air, his enthusiasm for computers, his irritation with bureaucracy, his belief in a clean political life. He wanted a computer in every school – previous politicians had struggled for 40 years with providing drinking water in every village. At least, the reasoning went, this guy had his priorities rooted in this century.

He was to let down many of his early supporters sensationally, by jettisoning many of the ideas and ideals others believed he possessed.

● In 1986, he backtracked when Muslim leaders condemned a Supreme Court judgment that allowed divorced Muslim women the right to financial maintenance from their estranged husbands. The Islamic clergy claimed the Court had interfered with Islam, and Gandhi exempted Indian Muslims from that Indian law. That was a blow to feminists and secularists.

● Later, when his defence minister, Vishwanath Pratap Singh, took his advice to remove corruption a bit too sincerely, first in the finance and then in the defence ministry, he abandoned him. That weakened the struggle for a clean public life.

● An aborted defamation bill, to curb press freedom, meant he lost the support of intellectuals and liberals.

● Finally, to the horror of secularists, he did not act in time to curb an incipient agitation launched by the BJP. The resurgent Hindu nationalist party wanted to build a temple to honour the Hindu god Rama at a site where some Hindus believed Rama was born millennia ago – it happened to be precisely the spot where the first Moghul emperor, Babar, had build a mosque, Babri Masjid, in the 16th century.

With *Ramayana* and *Mahabharata* mesmerising the masses, Gandhi unable to provide an intellectual counterpoint to the Hindu resurgence and the left discredited – the Soviet empire was unravelling, (in the southern state of Kerala at least two communist footsoldiers killed themselves, unable to bear the shame of the German Democratic Republic merging with the Federal Republic of Germany) – disenchantment with the trusted Indian model grew, leading to dismay and anger. That was translated into votes in 1989.

Since then, India has had three more parliamentary elections, with a fourth scheduled for September this year. (Elections must be held every five years). These parliaments have thrown up six different prime ministers, with only one of them, Congress's Narasimha Rao, completing a full term, from 1991 to 1996. And none of the six has commanded the majority of the parliament when elected.

The old consensus that governed India before 1989 – a liberal, socialist, secular democracy – has been breaking down, and the amorphous nature of the politics has lasted long enough to raise interesting, long-term questions about India's federal character. Does India want to be a strong, assertive nation, or is it a consensus-driven good neighbour? Will it remain a secular republic, or is it a Hindu state? Does India want to remain a liberal democracy, or is it turning right-wing? Is India still non-aligned, in a world where the old alignments have disappeared? Is India committed to the old socialist ethos, or is it really a capitalist, market-based economy in the making? And finally, who is an Indian – a Hindu, someone born in India, or someone who takes up Indian citizenship? What is India?

None of these questions will be answered in the next election, nor in the one after. The electoral confusion is so severe that it is unlikely that any party, or any leader, will be able to sway the electorate and obliterate the gnawing questions. The BJP, which ruled India for about a year before its parliamentary majority collapsed, had secured only 28% of the popular vote; given that only 55% of the voters voted in the last elections, it means only one in seven adult Indians had voted for that party. Since four out of five Indians are nominally Hindu, it shows, and offers the hope, that a large majority of Hindus haven't turned nationalist or fundamentalist. But it has meant a succession of weak governments at the centre.

Historically, a weak Delhi has not been good for India – the last such period was in the 1700s, when the Moghul empire was crumbling, the satraps were demanding independence and, in that void, the European colonists set up strongholds in preparation for their empires. The humiliation of that period is not lost: Ahmed Ali wrote a beautiful novel about it, *Twilight in Delhi*; and Vikram Chandra's *Red Earth and Pouring Rain* recreates the era masterfully.

Hindu nationalists claim the Moghul empire crumbled so easily because it was ruled by foreigners. Part of the resentment against Gandhi's Italian-born widow, Sonia, who may become prime minister if Congress returns to power in the September elections, stems from similar concerns – could someone who's not ethnically Indian lead India in these troubled times? Could she rally the troops if there were another war in Kargil? Would she stand up to international condemnation of India's human rights violations in Kashmir?

She will argue that it was the BJP's incompetent and weak government in Delhi that allowed Pakistani intruders to take up positions last year in the Himalayan heights, from which the Indian army repelled them at great cost this summer. And it is an achievement the BJP will, in turn, claim as proof of the success of its hardline policies.

But, paradoxically, a weak centre is good for business. When a senior Indian executive was asked how his life had changed since the economic liberalisation of Narasimha Rao in 1991, he said, with a sense of relief: 'I hardly fly to Delhi now.' Before liberalisation, business freedom was severely curbed. Vast areas of the economy were closed to big business and foreign collaborations were not allowed, unless it could be proved that the technology being imported was necessary and far superior to indigenous technology. A monopolies and restrictive trade practices commission regulated the activities of large corporations.

Companies weren't allowed to determine if they wanted to raise new capital, nor could they decide the premium they could charge on new shares. Foreign exchange regulations prevented Indian companies from investing abroad. Efficient companies that produced more than their permitted capacity were penalised. And the State reserved the right to compete with private business in everything, from producing butter to soft drinks, from bread to automobiles.

All that has now changed and, many Indians will agree, for the better – for India was a curious anomaly: a country with almost limitless political freedom, but weighed down by economic shackles. Indians could vote out governments, but weren't allowed to spend their money the way they liked, at home or abroad.

Since the reforms of 1991, industry has consolidated, and market forces have cleared away some of the inefficiencies in the private sector. Companies like the Tata group, Mahindra group, Birla group, are all seeking their core competencies, shedding businesses they don't need, building strengths in areas where they are most capable. The industrial scene is still in the state of churning, but analysts believe that in another decade the new Indian corporation will be more nimble and more efficient. Indian industry will be known for companies like Infosys, a crack NASDAQ-listed software company from Bangalore, rather than Hindustan Motors, which built the reliable, sturdy but dull and unchanging Ambassador cars to the same design for four decades.

It was Nehruvian socialism that restrained Indian business for nearly 50 years. If that's bad, could liberalism, secularism and even democracy also be bad? Nobody has seriously asked this question before, but Hindu nationalism, which is filling the intellectual void in India, is an important phenomenon precisely because it questions the basis of the Indian State.

That includes questioning non-alignment. Throughout the Cold War years, many Indians believed they were truly non-aligned. A look at India's voting record at the United Nations would, however, show that India was a close ally of the Soviet Union. The Soviets obliged by using the veto in India's favour when required; India reciprocated by providing intellectual arguments that supported some of the more egregious Soviet views during the Cold War.

Some Indian arguments had a sound moral basis and derived from older, non-interventionist concepts of sovereignty. But there were exceptions. India was the first country in the world to impose sanctions on South Africa, in 1948. India supported the Vietnamese invasion of Cambodia because it believed Pol Pot and the Khmer Rouge represented the greater evil. India backed the Palestinian struggle and African liberation movements, and opposed Cuba's isolation. But India failed to protest when the Soviets suppressed Solidarity in Poland, subjugated Czechoslovakia and Hungary; it didn't oppose Cuban forces in Angola (although it did oppose US intervention in Granada). Thus the non-alignment was certainly not even-handed. Indian bureaucrats argue India's hand was forced by the US; it was the US that wanted to open dialogue with China, and to do so it needed Pakistan as an ally. And in Cold War politics that meant opposing India. The two countries may be democracies but in realpolitik terms, their interests diverged.

During those years, the Soviet Union was India's largest trading partner. The oil industry was nationalised and new foreign brand names were banned – forcing Pepsi, when introduced in 1986, to be called Lehar Pepsi. India bought Polish machinery, Czech pistols and Soviet jets, and offered its tea, shoes and resorts in return, to settle a complicated debt that still depends on arcane mathematics, not the market value of the currencies.

When the Soviet Union collapsed and the eastern bloc became free, Narasimha Rao, perhaps the shrewdest Indian prime minister since Indira Gandhi, sardonically remarked: 'Decisions are easy when no options are left.' India had decided to embrace markets. Foreign investment hasn't lashed Indian shores with the ferocity that accompanied investment in East Asia, but Indians are smug these days. Their economy didn't suffer the fate of East Asia's in 1997.

Ambitious projects are announced, but the bureaucracy remains all-powerful, delaying decisions and overturning agreements, and spirited socialists continue to challenge the new economic order when it threatens, for instance, the ecology, peasant land rights or India's economic sovereignty.

Rao's market reforms divided Indian society in two – on one hand were those Indians, including upwardly mobile yuppies working at foreign banks, who couldn't have enough of reforms. They complained about inefficiency and government wastefulness; they yearned for the swanky cars, their children began eating out at McDonald's and Pizza Hut and they loved being seen in Levis jeans and RayBan glasses.

But there was another India – the kind personified by Shankar

SALIL TRIPATHI

Salgaonkar, who works as a chauffeur in Bombay. One afternoon, driving me to a bank's office in Nariman Point, he told me how the reforms had meant nothing for him: 'My boss has four credit cards and two airlines to choose from. What do I have to choose from? Coke and Pepsi!' he grumbled.

The reforms had bypassed him. He turned to the riff-raff bunch of the Shiv Sena, led by the Hitler-loving cartoonist-turned-politician, Bal Thackeray. Salgaonkar's boss, blaming the Congress for 50 years of decline, turned to the BJP, naively assuming that its leaders must be honest because they hadn't been in power for 45 years. Salgaonkar wanted the temple built in Ayodhya to commemorate Lord Rama; his boss wanted Pakistan to be taught a lesson. Together, they created the cocktail that allowed the coalition to support the first openly pro-Hindu government in India.

They felt the world was passing them by. India was not being taken note of. They felt India merited a bigger space in the international arena: spite being the largest democracy and the second-largest nation, it was not a permanent member of the UN Security Council. Countries protected by the US nuclear umbrella – Japan, Australia – had the gall to criticise India when it decided to test nuclear bombs in May 1998 without realising the dangers India faced across two borders – China and Pakistan, both nuclear states. India had opened its economy, deregulated its procedures, yet the rapid improvement in income levels experienced by East Asian states remained beyond India's grasp. Worse, China was the favourite destination for everyone's money. Why, when India had the English-speaking, scientifically-trained computer-literate manpower the world needed?

Something was rotten in the state of the world, not India, ran that logic. Perhaps the world would take notice, if India discarded the old order, and turned away from socialism, secularism and liberalism. Maybe India should look inwards, turn atavistic, and find solace in its Hindu ethos. It had its own fifth columnists within – the Muslims who prayed to an alien god, the Christians who converted the gullible tribals. A well-educated software engineer in an Indian office of a US-owned computer company could be heard telling a colleague in 1990: 'It is the innate desire of every Hindu that a temple should be built in Ayodhya at the site of the Muslim mosque.' Then, his colleagues laughed. Would they, in 1999?

And so it is that India has become strangely inward-looking when its economic reforms demand it look outward. Today, foreign funds are flowing again to India. India's gross domestic product growth is impressive. Its companies are posting record profits, and foreign investment approved since the 1991 reforms stands at over US$10 billion. Executives in Bangalore talk more with colleagues in the Silicon Valley than with the bureaucrats in Delhi; finance executives in Bombay know their counterparts in London and Hong Kong, not Calcutta. Some businessmen ask openly at parties in Bombay why Bombay can't be the capital of a united state of Gujarat and Maharashtra, two of India's most industrially-advanced states?

Such questioning reflects a deeply felt angst. It is a question of identity crisis. And India doesn't know the answer yet. Sunil Khilnani has called India an idea. That it is. And it is one that millions believed in instinctively in the 1950s and 1960s, even up to the 1970s. But Indira Gandhi's Emergency jolted the democratic foundations; Rao's reforms destroyed the socialist consensus; and the destruction of Babri Masjid shook the secular foundations. Maybe India was a dream, not an idea; a dream, as Salman Rushdie wrote in *Midnight's Children*, that 'everybody had agreed to dream'.

Now India has woken up to a different world. And many Indians want to rewrite the rules. It is the failure to understand those foundations that's prompting many Indians to demand that the government revoke the special status granted to Kashmir, India's only Muslim-majority state. They don't realise that doing so would nullify the legal basis for Kashmir's accession to India in 1948. But these days, few Indians have time to debate such niceties. They argue that India is a secular country, so Kashmir being a Muslim-majority state should not matter.

Yet, some of them question the right of Sonia Gandhi to run for office. Italian-born Sonia married Rajiv Gandhi in the late 1960s, becoming an Indian citizen nearly two decades later. Many Indians ask why she took so long to change her citizenship. Others demand to know her qualifications to rule India. (Such questions weren't asked of other offspring littering the Indian political scene.) Still others, bordering on racism, ask whether a foreign-born citizen can rule India.

The question is an important one, and Gandhi hasn't helped her case by refusing to grant press interviews; by refusing to be probed. She has made thunderous speeches in which she has claimed she is genuinely committed to India, that she is the daughter-in-law of India. That she is; her family's role in Indian politics is a long, illustrious and controversial one. India allows naturalisation (Mother Teresa was a citizen) and naturalised Indians can run for office. Instead of seeing virtue in such liberal policies, some Indians now believe that's wrong because the US, for example, doesn't allow naturalised Americans to run for the White House. As Ashutosh Varshneya, a South Asia expert at Columbia University points out, unlike Germany, India doesn't grant citizenship based on ethnic or race-based grounds; for centuries it has absorbed cultures and influences rather than separated them. The drive to deny Sonia Gandhi her right to run for office is contrary to a culture that has believed in *Vasudhaiva Kutumbakam* (The world is my family) and a nation that believes in 'unity in diversity'. This xenophobia, this separatist, identity-based politics, ultimately stems from deeply felt insecurity, sense of hurt and wounded pride.

How India resolves this dilemma – of liberal democracy versus religion-based nationalism – is important, not just for India, but for the world. For the idea of India, as Khilnani argued, is an important one, a noble one – where anyone can become an Indian, everyone votes, and anyone could become the prime minister.

In 1984, within hours of Indira Gandhi's assassination, Conor Cruise O'Brien noted: 'India's democracy is one of the great achievements of this century.' It would be a failure of epic proportions if it changes its character fundamentally in the next. It is time for midnight's children to grow up and stop dreaming about a past that doesn't exist.❑

Salil Tripathi is a regular contributor to Index. He is a writer based in London

JOHN GITTINGS

Chinese whispers

The 10th aniversary of the Tiananmen massacre passed quietly enough but the desire for change and for democracy is as strong as ever

The 10 anniversary of the 3/4 June 1989 Beijing Massacre was, for the western media, an anti-climax. Nothing happened around Tiananmen Square (the square itself was sealed off 'under repair') except for two protests by lone individuals. This was not unexpected: the dissident movement had been severely harassed in the run-up to the anniversary. The so-called 'Beijing spring' of 1998, in which more diverse voices were heard at least in the capital, had been succeeded by a winter of repression, particularly against the organisers in the provinces of a would-be China Democracy Party. It was hard to recall that, less than a year before, Bill Clinton was congratulating himself on the famous debate with President Jiang Zemin in which he actually mentioned the words democracy and Tibet live on Chinese TV (though few were watching because the programme had not been announced in advance).

Yet the most striking event which threw the non-event of the anniversary into perspective was the outburst of rage, just a month before, that followed the US bombing of the Chinese embassy in Belgrade. While this was to some extent stage-managed by the Chinese authorities, their efforts were directed as much to channelling popular anger as to kindling it. Students from universities that had marched for democracy 10 years before now took to the streets to denounce 'US hegemonism'. The class of 1999 appeared to have very different values from the class of 1989.

It was tempting to conclude, as many outside commentators did, that the spirit of Tiananmen Square was in some sense now an anachronism.

The sacrifices made by the tiny minority who continued to struggle were acknowledged; the suffering of those in jail (including many hundreds still serving savage sentences handed out in 1989 or soon after) was recognised; the future dangers faced by a political system that delivered economic reform while stifling parallel political change were pointed out. But the general conclusion was that, for better or worse, over the past decade 'China has changed' into a very different sort of place. A sense of moral distancing was encouraged by the reports of the anti-US student demonstrators of today eating at the ubiquitous McDonald's, or aspiring to gain graduate scholarships to the USA. And some of the biggest student names from 10 years ago were now thriving in exile in the computer software or financial services industries. Those dissidents abroad who continued to be politically active were also at each other's throats – in one famous incident, literally so, on the floor of a congressional committee room. The overall effect was to dim the relevance of 1989 and even the memories – except for the now-clichéd image of the young man who stopped the tanks. The issue of political reform as a current topic in China was blurred, beyond saying in very general terms that someday, somehow, it is still needed.

There was another strand of analysis that helped to cast Tiananmen Square as an epic event but one that definitely belonged to history. This was the argument that much of what the students in 1989 were seeking had now been achieved: China was a more diverse society in which most of the freedoms could now be enjoyed, at least informally and at least by the majority who were not in some form of prison. Again, the effect was to diminish the struggle for democracy: if people could now have foreign holidays, buy sex aids at least in the bigger cities, purchase their own apartments, aspire to buy a car, complain about officialdom, then life clearly was not so bad.

It is not the first time that China's democracy movement has been subtly downgraded. The brave efforts of the activists of Democracy Wall in 1979 – 80 (the direct precursor of 1989) were also put down by many foreigners – especially by diplomats who valued China as an anti-Soviet ally, and business interests who valued the Chinese market. It is also true that China has indeed changed and in many ways for the better. Most Chinese think so (although there is probably an equal number in the disadvantaged rural areas who would disagree). And most people's memories of 1989 are dim, distorted or, in the case of half the

Beijing students building the 'Goddess of Democracy and Freedom' for erection in Tiananmen Square, 29 May 1989 – Credit: Patrik Zachman/Magnum

Michael Jackson, Mickey Mouse and the man-who-faced-the-tanks

A peculiar price of fame in this era of transnational mass communication is that the words and deeds of people who happen to catch the eye of the media can instantly take on complex and globally symbolic lives of their own. Replicated and appropriated in a dizzying array of electronic and print media, a phrase or even a gesture that attracts the attention of CNN or the BBC can end up being put to a variety of uses.

We still do not know the name of the lone hero who stood his ground before a line of tanks on 5 June 1989 near Tiananmen Square, but when a camera recorded his act he instantly became one of the most celebrated figures of our times. His body has appeared on T-shirts as well as on posters promoting documentary films. He has been referred to in speeches by everyone from British politicians to rock stars on the other side of the Atlantic and dissidents in the former Soviet empire. On the Internet, there are websites devoted to Chinese struggles for democracy that display his image, others that invite you to purchase a commemorative photograph of him. Memories of his stand-off with the tanks of the People's Liberation Army (PLA) have even been worked into ads for Benetton. There has been at least one feature film, a futuristic movie by Wim Wenders, that includes a visual allusion to his famous act, and an exhibition made up of nothing but a series of photographs of his confrontation. His picture has graced the covers of several books and he was selected by *Time* as one of the hundred most memorable individuals of the century. When the Walt Disney Corporation was in dispute with the Chinese authorities, he assumed the image of Mickey Mouse in US cartoons.

Perhaps the oddest appropriation of this anonymous act of heroism came several years ago during a world tour by pop star Michael Jackson. *New York Times* music critic Jon Pareles, describes a surreal moment in Jackson's rendering of 'Earth Song' when the singer assumes the pose of a man calling on advancing forces to stop. This, Parales notes, was clearly meant to make members of the audience think of the man-who-stopped-the-tanks and was evidence of the star's penchant for 'shamelessly restaging history as self-aggrandising entertainment'. It can also be seen as but one of the many strange twists in the history of a political symbol.

But in many ways, the most disturbing abuse of the image of the man-who-stopped-the-tanks is one that took place in China itself that same year. When state television was ordered to figure out ways of justifying the army's use of force against civilian protesters and onlookers, Chinese audiences were soon being shown some of the same shots that Americans and Europeans saw on network broadcasts – but with a very different commentary. The fact that the tanks swerved and did not kill the unnamed man, despite his efforts to keep them from doing their job, was offered as 'proof' that the PLA had shown great restraint in dealing with the 'troublemakers' and 'lunatics' with whom it had to contend. 'Anyone with common sense can see,' the narrator comments, 'that if our tanks were determined to move on, this lone scoundrel could never have stopped them.' The precise fate of the man who stopped the tanks may, like his identity, remain a mystery, but we can be certain that he did not emerge from his brush with fame unscathed. We are not sure whether he was a student (as many have assumed) or a worker (as others have speculated). We do know, however, that he was taken into custody in 1989 during the crackdown that followed the massacres and, given his lack of visibility since then, it seems likely he was quietly executed soon after. □

Jeffrey N Wasserstrom is an associate professor of history at Indiana University. His books include Student Protests in Twentieth-Century China: the View from Shanghai *(Stanford University Press) and the forthcoming* Human Rights and Revolutions *(Rowman and Littlefield, 2000), which he is co-editing with Lynn Hunt and Marilyn Young* population who were only children then, non-existent.

But to couch the analysis in these terms is to miss the main point: it is precisely in the area of free political expression that there has been least change – and in some respects things have gone backwards. It obscures the more subtle efforts now being made, within as well as outside the established Party framework, to revive ideas of reform. Not every intellectual simply wants to publish a profitable book; not every Party cadre merely wants to gain a share of the cake of corruption. Focusing on the transformation of former activists into monarchs of the Web is entertaining but beside the point. This is not the first time exiled campaigners have fallen into the trap of factional infighting and become irrelevant to internal politics. The focus should be rather on those within China, whether they are named dissidents or anonymous sacked state employees, over-taxed farmers, struggling pensioners, cheated investors or any of the other social groups who express their discontent.

This populist aspect of social protest today in China is not so different from the spirit of 1989. It may not have been a popular movement in a mass sense, but it certainly struck a popular chord in many levels of society. I remember meeting two diplomats at the Chinese embassy in London when the students first occupied Tiananmen Square. 'Isn't it tremendous news?' they asked excitedly. The movement developed links for the first time between Party reformers and non-Party activists in a dynamic combination; it soon acquired support from newly emerging worker's organisations.

Most strikingly for anyone who walked the streets of Beijing at that time, it gained the backing of the ordinary people of Beijing. It was the *shimin*, the citizens, who staffed the barricades after martial law was proclaimed, who shamed the army for two weeks into remaining on the outskirts and who provided the largest number of casualties when the armed units eventually smashed their way into the centre. For the Deng Xiaoping leadership, the threat of popular participation was probably a greater threat than that presented by the massed students or even by the presence of workers. Where the movement spread to the provinces, it attracted not only local students but a sometimes unruly element – as in the more violent demonstrations in Xian and Chengdu. This populist tinge was typified in the memorable slogan of the big marches in the first days of May: '*Renmin wansui*' (long live the people!') This is not a slogan in conformity with the 'top-down' concept of socialist democracy though its rare uses have been significant. Mao Zedong used it when reviewing the Red Guards in Tiananmen Square in 1966 – in his own most populist phase. The *People's Daily* used it exceptionally in a December 1978 editorial that legitimised the anti-Gang of Four mass demonstration in the same square two years earlier in April 1976 – until then labelled 'counter-revolutionary'. (The editorial also implied approval for the Democracy Wall then being launched in Beijing.) Otherwise it is the Party, not the People, who are supposed to Live for Ever.

The protest of 1989 was, therefore, always much more diverse than the usual label 'students, democracy movement' suggests. And its more diverse aspects are not as anachronistic as that of the elite student activism now dispersed to Princeton and California. At one end of the political spectrum, there is a renewed discourse within the Party that can be called 'pro-reform', although it is more careful in how it expresses itself than in the pre-1989 period when 'political salons' thrived in Beijing. When this new mood attracted attention in early 1998 it was given the misleading label of a 'Beijing spring' – which then turned to winter. In fact, the dialogue has continued (though it may temporarily have been silenced by the ultra-nationalist din of protest against the Belgrade embassy bombing).

In public print, the argument is mostly indirect. A spate of new books in the late 1990s has recounted the earlier persecution of intellectuals as 'Rightists' in 1957 and analysed the disasters of the Great Leap Forward. Others have eulogised the former Party secretary-general, Hu Yaobang, for rehabilitating the 'Rightists' in the early 1980s. They omit to say, but the readers will already know, that Hu was sacked under hardline pressure in 1987 and that his death two years later brought the students into Tiananmen Square. Books by two controversial journalists, Ma Licheng and Ling Zhiyun, tackle more delicate contemporary issues. In 1998 they upset the establishment with *Crossing Swords*, satirising the polemics of the Party dogmatists who still wield influence. A year later their new book, *Crying Out*, analysed the 'five voices' in current Chinese politics. These, they say, are reformism, dogmatism, nationalism, feudalism and – democracy.

Some subjects are ignored, notably the actual events of 1989. But the social ills of 1999, from rampant corruption and rural oppression to deficiencies in health and education and the yawning income gap, are analysed in serious academic studies often based on field work or sampling techniques. A new vogue for investigative journalism has also been fostered by the new popular tabloids. Many of these are offshoots of more politically correct dailies controlled by the Party. The front-runner is the *Nanfang Ribao (Southern Daily)*, now sold nationwide. The *Beijing Qingnian Bao (Beijing Youth Newspaper)* is the most adventurous paper in the capital; the *China Youth Newspaper* also has a reputation for reportage. Popular police and legal journals, published in many provinces, offer a sensational mixture of sex and crime but include some serious investigation. It may be driven by competition for readers, but the result is to throw light on dark corners of bureaucratic incompetence, nepotism and graft that have never before been revealed in such detail in the public press. Muck-raking journalists are sometimes harassed by local officials or even detained illegally.

At the other end of the spectrum of current political culture, there is an increasing number of social groups prepared to mobilise, protest, and exercise pressure in defence of their interests. These are not a unified mass movement and their numbers have been exaggerated in the claims of some dissidents abroad. But they are sufficiently widespread to alarm the government in Beijing which, at the National People's Congress in March 1999, urged the provinces to find ways of dealing with local dissent. The usual method has been to build up the police and security forces (which then impose an even greater drain on local resources that is met by further extortion from the peasants). The administration of Premier Zhu Rongji more perceptively urges the bureaucracy to tackle the grievances instead and avoid the traditional resort to repression. Hundreds, probably thousands, of small-scale peasant protests occur every year, particularly in provinces of the interior such as Hubei, Hunan, Sichuan, Guangxi, Anhui and Jiangxi, where corruption is not offset by rising prosperity. But urban workers thrown out of jobs before their time have also found that demonstrating is the only way to secure the meagre lay-off benefits to which they are entitled. Though these are unconnected, they represent a large pool of discontent that is motivated by a deep-seated belief in the need for social justice – sometimes expressed with reference to the 'socialist' past and, at others, more simply in terms of self-evident human values. Such protests have a rough edge to them and there have been ugly scenes, usually unreported.

For the government in Beijing, the lesson of Tiananmen Square remains as valid today as it was when spelled out by the 'Party elders' who gathered around Deng Xiaoping and sent in the tanks. It is that they must not lose control. Deng's solution, after several years of political stagnation following the Beijing Massacre, was to kick-start China's economic revolution into a new, more generalised phase that could, it was hoped, distribute benefits more widely. This has evidently succeeded to some extent: urban standards of living have improved and a minority of peasants have also been enriched. The Asian economic crisis administered a severe jolt at a time when the negative implications of reform, particularly in the attempt to shake out the state industrial sector, were beginning to be felt. There is still a fairly widespread sense of commitment to the status quo – or at least of fear that any radical change could lead to uncontainable *luan* or 'disorder'. But there is also a general distaste for the seamy side of reform even among many who, in order to get one, are obliged to take or give favours. Here, too, the national government is making strenuous efforts to root out corruption and its consequences – dramatically manifested in the late 1990s by a series of accidents in which bridges collapsed and boilers burst because shoddy contractors had obtained the work corruptly.

The frontal challenge to the Communist Party by a few single-minded (sometimes obsessive) individuals seeking to establish a China Democracy Party is variously seen as heroic and misguided. It is probably both, though the repression it has attracted shows the regime in the worst possible light. Change to the political system will not come from this quarter but from the interaction of much more complex and inchoate forces responding to social injustice and economic hardship.

After 1989, many observers (including this writer) believed it likely that the Communist Party would collapse within a few years. This was not only an incorrect forecast, it also focused too much on the upper reaches of Chinese political culture. It is possible even now to visualise a set of circumstances in which the Party would consume itself, a vacuum would appear at the centre – and the people would again flock to Tiananmen Square. Yet the real arena for democracy is not in the square or even in Beijing but in communities throughout China, both in the increasingly autonomous world of intellectuals and among the – also increasingly – complex social formations at the grassroots. In July, the banning of the quasi-religious *Falun Gong* (Art of the Wheel of Buddhist Law) cult brought one such formation to surprising prominence. The organisation was denounced by the government with a ferocity unparalleled since the witchhunt 10 years earlier against the activists of Tiananmen Square. The *Falun Gong* has apparently attracted a large number of Party members and it was alleged that the mass demonstration the cult staged on 25 April this year, outside the headquarters of the Party leadership, was organised by two Party cadres. The crackdown that followed, said to have been organised personally by President Jiang Zemin, seemed to be excessive. Yet the *Falun Gong* presented a real challenge to the Party's monopoly of organisational power. Future challenges to the regime may well come from other unpredictable social formations that are quietly building up their strength.

This does not necessarily mean that democracy in the formal sense will be seen to be irrelevant when the opportunity comes for new political initiatives. The Chinese people have been accused since early this century of either not knowing about democracy or not wanting it. This is not only a patronising view but it ignores the extent to which an idea can be grasped when its time has come. The Indonesian elections of May 1999, when millions of Indonesians plunged with enthusiasm into organising and participating in the country's first real election for over four decades, shows the immense potential to be realised when people feel that at last their voice will count. That moment is a long way off in China – but that does not mean that politics will stand still till then.

The veteran journalist Liu Binyan, in exile since the late 1980s but for decades a vigorous critic from within, has come to a similar conclusion in the final issue of *China Focus*, the bulletin he published from 1992 to 1999 at the Princeton China Initiative (see also *Index* 1/1997). After the Beijing Massacre, Liu recalls, he estimated that 'within a short period of time political change would occur in China. But none of my predictions came true. After 1992 [when Deng re-started the economic reforms], I found myself facing an entirely different China.' Liu acknowledges that the new policies were immensely popular, establishing a tacit social contract between the government and society. He did not foresee that many intellectuals as well as bureaucrats and the *nouveau riche* would become 'a new conservative force'. Nevertheless, Liu pins his hopes for the future on the even newer forces now emerging: the new radicalism of younger intellectuals who are not afraid to expose the darker side of society, and the emergence of essentially non-political organisations among ordinary people.

Liu's conclusion is one that all commentators should accept – with humility: 'While observing China,' he writes, 'we must pay sufficient attention to the characteristics of the society and the people.' It is hard to believe that the current political structure, still in its essentials not so different from that which has ruled China for the past five decades, can remain recognisably the same for yet one more decade. It is changing in ways both obvious and less so. But where it reaches in the end really does depend on the people. ❑

John Gittings *is East Asia correspondent for the* Guardian *and the* Observer, *currently Hong Kong based. His latest book,* China Through the Sliding Door *(Simon & Schuster, London 1999, £7.99) is a selection of his reports from China over the past 30 years*

ALEX DE WAAL

War trap

The Cold War was never cold in Africa. Militarisation, repression and outright war during the Cold War decades condemned Africa to a cycle from which it seems unable to escape

The commonest cause of war is war. Since the end of the Cold War, the number of armed conflicts in Africa has remained stubbornly high. Today it is about the same as in 1989, or 1979 – that is, outrageously high. In some areas, conflicts have even got worse. During the 1990s there have been perhaps 15 new or renewed wars across sub-Saharan Africa, dashing the hopes of those who believed that the end of superpower antagonism would see the emergence of a new peace across the continent. The weakness of African states, political and ethnic divisions, competition for scarce resources: all have played their role in sparking and sustaining conflicts. But, taking a broad look at these conflicts, a single factor stands out. All but one of these wars have erupted in a country that was at war in the previous decade, or had a neighbour at war.

Metaphors mislead. War does not 'erupt' like a volcano or 'spill over' like a flooded river. It is not akin to a natural disaster. War is begun by individuals, usually men, who at the very minimum are not averse to fighting, and often are eager to do so. They may not calculate the outcomes of their actions – in fact, it is probable that no war in modern history has had the consequences predicted by those who launched it – but they are ready for the gamble. Moreover, often it is a small group of individuals, perhaps just one, who plays this critical role. Understanding contemporary war in Africa means looking both at the big picture, and focusing on the men who start wars.

The war trap means that the proxy wars fought by the superpowers from the 1960s to the 1980s continue to work their deadly logic on the African continent. Exactly how that logic works varies from case to case – and there are important exceptions to the general rule – but there is a common reality. The Cold War introduced so much organised violence into the African continent that it may be a generation before its consequences die away.

The saddest and most archetypal war is Angola. Beginning as an anti-colonial struggle in the 1960s, this war metamorphosed into a Cold War hot war, as each superpower chose its client. Internal rivalries were exploited by the Americans and Soviets for their geo-strategic interests – and the Cold War confrontation was exploited by their local clients in pursuit of their ambitions. A moment of hope for peace occurred with an agreement followed by elections in 1991 – 2. But this was dashed when Jonas Savimbi was denied his ambition of taking the presidency and resumed his insurrection. Since then, successive rounds of fighting have been ever-more destructive and ever-more pointless – and, unlike Mozambique, Liberia or Somalia, Angola's immense mineral wealth (oil and diamonds) means that each side can finance a high-technology war, apparently ad infinitum. Ideology has become an irrelevance. Angolan citizens are weary of this war, not so their leaders.

Today, the most destructive war in Africa, if not the world, is between Ethiopia and Eritrea. In massive assaults on one another's fortified positions along their common border, tens of thousands of young people have been killed and maimed, and two near-destitute countries have bought tanks, artillery and jet fighters to pound one another. And for what? The stated war aims of each side are a few miles of disputed scrubby land, scarcely big enough to be a graveyard for all those who have died trying to win it. In May-June 1998, a border skirmish escalated into a full-scale confrontation with air strikes, followed by months of rearming and then immense ground battles beginning in February this year.

An analysis of the rights and wrongs of this immense and tragic conflict is beyond the scope of this article. The war has nothing to do with ideology. The only obvious Cold War legacy is that both sides are utilising – in large part – arsenals provided by the Soviets to the former Ethiopian government in its communist days. Unfortunately, the Soviet preference for manufacturing simple and sturdy tanks and artillery pieces means that equipment from the 1940s and 1950s has outlasted the state that made it.

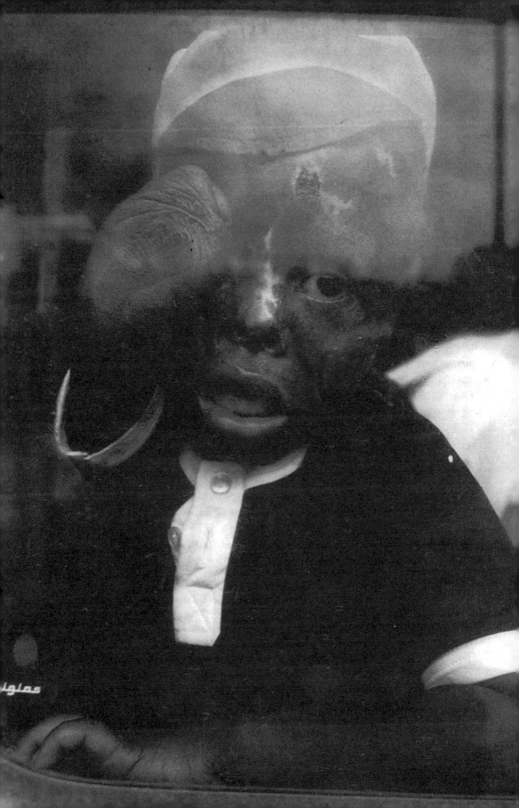

But a major factor in the rapid ratcheting up into full-scale war was that both leaderships were ready to threaten, and use, military force, and neither was ready to back down in the face of threats. This is surely related to the fact that both leaderships emerged from sustained armed struggles themselves just seven years earlier, and were still partly on a war footing facing down armed threats from neighbours including Sudan and Somalia. Their threshold for starting a war was alarmingly low – one manifestation of the war trap.

Meanwhile, this civil war has rekindled the flames in Somalia, with Eritrea arming certain groups and Ethiopia launching a full-scale invasion and backing its own clients.

The internationalised war in Zaire/Democratic Republic of Congo is another case. What might appear to be a wholly new war is in fact a direct bequest of the Cold War. For decades, US patronage enabled a fantastically venal dictator to hold his country together, achieving a measure of 'peace' at the cost of decay and fragmentation. But the internal conflicts in Zaire were merely frozen, while the government – or to be precise, the factions around the president – lavishly sponsored conflicts in neighbouring countries including Rwanda and Angola. These were ultimately self-defeating strategies. By the mid-1990s, Mobutu's readiness to destabilise his neighbours backfired, as an array of antagonised neighbours (led by Rwanda) and their friends combined to overthrow him. Then, no-one in Zaire would stand up and fight for the discredited despot – but neither would they unite around an alternative.

Meanwhile, the inheritance of years of armament, and the presence of so many foreign armies on Congolese soil, has made a solution to the DR Congo's plight exceptionally elusive. The conflict, too, has generated its own destructive logic. The vicious internal war in Congo (Brazzaville) in 1997, the resumption of fighting in Angola, continuing destabilisation of Rwanda and Uganda, and threats to the stability of Zambia and Zimbabwe can all be traced directly to the lack of any form of security in DR Congo. The one positive thing that can be said is that at least this war demonstrates the impossibility of a piecemeal solution: the wars are all interlinked and must be resolved together.

There is a single African exception to the 'wars before' rule: Liberia. Here, instead of opting for the customary coup, Charles Taylor sought to fight his way to power through rural insurrection. A political-military entrepreneur *par excellence*, Taylor deployed low-cost social technologies, including conspicuous atrocity and the recruitment of child soldiers, to sow violent discord and mobilise fighters. His manipulation of ethnicity destabilised Liberia, belatedly and perversely demonstrating the logic of Che Guevara-style focoism used for purely cynical ends. Frustrated in his ambitions by the Nigerian-led West African intervention force, Taylor then ignited war in neighbouring Sierra Leone as well. Once started, such wars generate their own logic. In their own way, they are total wars: the social technologies involved are all-encompassing and bring all of society to the battle front. Unlike conventional, state-mobilised wars, which may have spin-off benefits in terms of social cohesion and state consolidation, these wars are purely destructive, a form of primary annihilation.

Taylor's invasion of Liberia has, therefore, plunged a large area of West Africa into its own war trap. This is unusual in Africa because it is not of Cold War vintage, but the implications are the same.

The war trap is not new, nor unique to Africa. Warmaking is a profession, a career. However disparate the natures and aims of war, soldiers have much in common. In societies at war, soldiers are given esteem and reward; afterwards, countries are faced with the challenge of demobilisation. After every major war this century, the world has been flooded with unemployed soldiers. The post-Cold War demobilisations are no exception. Military Professional Resources Inc. soaks up retired US army officers; Executive Outcomes and the network of companies it has spawned have given jobs to many otherwise unemployable former South African soldiers and intelligence operatives; the dispersal of the international brigades of the Afghan *mujahidin* has provided trained terrorists and guerrillas to every Islamist cause from Kashmir to Algeria (see **pxxx**). Serbs and Croats are among the latest additions to this market; some are merely plying their destructive trade for money alone, others still nurse political or ideological agendas.

The same problem is replicated in every country or district where there has been a war. Schools are often the largest sources of recruits for guerrilla armies: students join up with the dream of resuming their education when their land is liberated. Others join from economic frustrations: their land is seized, their chances of employment eliminated. Return to civilian life can be a rude awakening – especially when international donors insist that economic 'adjustment' be implemented at the same time as peace and reconciliation, so that tens of thousands of hopeful ex-soldiers enter the labour market and demand education just at the moment when their prospects are poorest. Little surprise that banditry or mercenarism are attractive options.

The human residues of former wars provide the raw material for political entrepreneurs wanting to return to the bush. But leaders are needed to turn frustrations into organised insurrection. Unfortunately, war, like politics, throws up more potential leaders than there are positions to fill. War always leaves unmet promises and armouries of grievance. So there are likely to be former officers ready to return to leading an army in the field.

The war in Sudan started in precisely this way in the 1980s as ambitious and frustrated commanders of the first civil war in Sudan (concluded in 1972) remobilised disgruntled veterans and youth and launched a civil war that has brought ruin to southern Sudan. Their cause may have been just, but the sheer devastation that has followed was surely not in the minds of the mutineers 16 years ago. The Sudan People's Liberation Army was founded with the aim of creating a united, secular socialist Sudan – all three aims more distant now than when the war started. The government of Sudan fights for an Islamic State, but it, too, is finding that the longer the war continues, the more remote its goal. At the beginning of the war, the US supported the pro-West Khartoum government; by the late 1990s, it was verbally supporting the opposition. Irrespective of US alignment, the war seems insoluble.

Similarly, the war in Somalia, another Cold War orphan: veterans of the failed invasion of Ethiopia in 1977 provided a ready-mobilised army for a military entrepreneur such as General Mohamed Aidid to pursue his ambitions. When Aidid was killed in 1996, the democratic and prosperous Somalia on whose behalf he had launched his insurrection was further away than ever.

The infamous mercenary corporation Executive Outcomes is a variant on the story: its directors seek only profit, not political power. EO began life as an arm of the clandestine South African destabilisation strategy, working for the Civil Cooperation Bureau that organised covert activities such as the assassination of ANC leaders. After the CCB was closed and apartheid's counter-insurgency and destabilisation strategies abandoned, EO simply moved into the commercial sphere, landing contracts with the governments of Angola and Sierra Leone. EO's reputation is probably out of proportion to its actual activities, but it is the most flamboyant member of an extensive network of private military companies that includes MPRI and Defence Systems Limited. EO was formally closed in January 1999, but its numerous offspring, such as Sandline, continue in business.

The 'blowback' from the CIA's massive support to the Afghan *mujahidin* is even more immense and equally serious for Africa. The likes of Osama bin Laden are the direct legacy of the US policy of pouring arms into Afghanistan and training all comers in the most sophisticated and deadly techniques of destruction. The extremist Islamist government in Khartoum is a cousin of this US misadventure. In the 1970s and early 1980s, the State Department encouraged the Sudanese National Islamic Front as an acceptable, modern, conservative force; a reliable ally in its regional anti-communist strategy and one that gave a more liberal gloss to political Islam than the Saudis and Iranians. Frustrated with the inept leadership of Sudan's elected government (1986 – 9), Washington also sent clear signals that it would not oppose a military coup in that country. But what it got, in June 1989, was a military-Islamist coalition that quickly became one of its favourite objects of hate, a relationship that culminated in the cruise missile attack on the *al Shifa* pharmaceutical plant in August 1998. (In a remarkable display of state-of-the-art intelligence, the US neatly destroyed an innocent factory, leaving the actual chemical weapons installations – whose location was known to every Khartoum taxi driver – unscathed.) Meanwhile, Sudanese citizens have laboured under a vile dictatorship for the entire post-Cold War period.

Perhaps the most significant legacy of war is that it legitimises violence as a form of political activity. Nobody starts a long war: all long wars are short wars that did not stick to the script. But for those who have engaged in war before, fighting can still appear legitimate, not to mention fulfilling. Those who won the previous war believe they can do it again; those who failed believe that they can remedy their own or their superiors' mistakes next time round. As the Eritrea-Ethiopia war demonstrates, the smallest spark can ignite a conflagration that can consume whole nations. As Liberia shows, a single able ambitious man, determined to ruin or rule a state, can do both.

Once started, war has its own monstrous dynamic: escalation,

Simon Davies on
PRIVACY

Patricia Williams on
RACE

JOURNALISM

INTERNET

FREE SPEECH

...all in INDEX

SUBSCRIBE & SAVE

UK and overseas

○ **Yes! I want to subscribe to *Index*.**

❐ 1 year (6 issues)   £39   Save 28%
❐ 2 years (12 issues)   £74   Save 31%
❐ 3 years (18 issues)   £102   **You save 37%**

Name

Address

                                                 B9B5

£ _____ enclosed. ❐ Cheque (£) ❐ Visa/MC ❐ Am Ex ❐ Bill me
(*Outside of the UK, add £6 a year for foreign postage*)

Card No.

Expiry   Signature

❐ I do not wish to receive mail from other companies.

INDEX
✉ Freepost: INDEX, 33 Islington High Street, London N1 9BR
☎ (44) 171 278 2313   Fax: (44) 171 278 1878
e tony@indexoncensorship.org

SUBSCRIBE & SAVE

North America

○ **Yes! I want to subscribe to *Index*.**

❐ 1 year (6 issues) $52   Save 21%
❐ 2 years (12 issues) $96   Save 27%
❐ 3 years (18 issues) $135   **You save 32%**

Name

Address

                                                 B9B5

$ _____ enclosed. ❐ Cheque ($) ❐ Visa/MC ❐ Am Ex ❐ Bill me

Card No.

Expiry   Signature

❐ I do not wish to receive mail from other companies.

INDEX, 708 Third Avenue, 8th Floor, New York, NY 10017
☎ (44) 171 278 2313   Fax: (44) 171 278 1878
e tony@indexoncensorship.org

prolongation, dragging in other countries, degrading morality. The logic of war consumes everything. It poisons normal political discourse and human rationality. The fear for contemporary Africa is that the inflammable legacies of so many ongoing or suspended conflicts will create more destructive wars in the decade to come.

The African continent witnessed so much armed conflict during the 1960s, 1970s and 1980s that it produced an entire generation for whom organised violence was a way of life and a normal means of political mobilisation. The goals and ideologies associated with these conflicts were secondary to the simple fact of warfare itself, so casually started by the superpowers and their clients. The repercussions of this extraordinary level of armament, division, destruction and socialisation into war live on in Africa's contemporary war trap. It will take many years, and a concerted effort by Africans and the international community, to reverse this state of affairs. ❏

Alex de Waal is the director of Justice Africa. He has been a writer on war, famine and human rights in Africa for 15 years. He lives in London

ALAIN LABROUSSE

Uncle Sam's junk

US manipulation of the drugs trade to fund its covert operations and proxy wars during the Cold War created a fine legacy for the post-war inheritors of the business

It was US president Richard Nixon, shocked by the tens of thousands of GIs returning from Vietnam as heroin addicts, who coined the phrase 'the war on drugs' in 1971. Throughout the war, the CIA had turned a blind eye to the trafficking of its allies in the region and the addiction of at least 10% of its army was an inevitable consequence.

The connection between military adventures, wars and drugs is as old as humanity's use of 'mind altering substances'. Between the 11th and 13th centuries, the *hashisheen* or Assassins, members of a fanatical religious sect, waged war on the caliphs in Baghdad as well as on the crusaders from the West under the influence, or promise, of hashish. In the middle of the last century, French and British imperialist adventurers profited hugely from the Opium Wars.

But no country in the world has ever made such constant and systematic use of drugs as the USA. They were a weapon in the armoury of its anti-communist crusade throughout the Cold War. This is as true of the Cold War proper – the 15 years that followed WWII – as of the period characterised by the confrontation of the blocks after the Cuban missile crisis in October 1962.

In South East Asia, US narco-politics began with the operations of the Office of Strategic Service (OSS) in WW II. Following the Japanese occupation of Burma, the OSS, forerunner of the CIA, set up local anti-Japanese guerrilla groups across the border in neighbouring Assam. These were financed by the opium trade, without which, says the commander of 'Detachment 101', William R Peers, 'there would have been no operation'. When the Chinese Communists defeated the

Kuomintang in 1949, the remnants of its 93rd division under General Li Mi retreated to the Shan state in northern Burma where, with the help of Taiwan and the CIA, they were to spearhead an invasion of China from the south. The nationalists developed the production of opium by the local tribes to pay for the operation. In the end, the invasion came to nothing and the KMT troops were repatriated to Taiwan by the UN; some units, swollen with local recruits, settled in Thailand. In the early-1960s, with the help of chemists from Hong Kong, the KMT began to produce morphine and high-quality, 90-99% pure, 'white' heroin. This was the beginning of the change from the production of a few dozen tonnes of opium a year for traditional local use in the 1940s to the production of 2,500 tonnes by the end of the 1990s; for the first half of this decade, Burma was the world's leading supplier.

In Vietnam, the French army financed its covert operations thanks to the opium and heroin trade via the Corsican network known as the 'French Connection'. The CIA inherited the trade and used it to finance its own secret army drawn from the Hmong (known locally as Meo) tribes. By 1965, this numbered 300,000 troops.

The drugs-money-arms nexus throughout the Caribbean and Central America long predates the Sandinista victory in Nicaragua. Before the Colombians moved in, the drugs market in Miami was the fief of exiled Cubans, many of whom had taken part in the CIA's abortive invasion of the Bay of Pigs in 1961. In 1971, over 100 of them were rounded up in Operation Eagle; according to attorney general John Mitchel, their network was responsible for 30% of the heroin market in the USA.

When Congress used the Boland Amendment to veto all US military aid to anti-Sandinista forces – the *contras* – between October 1984 and October 1986, the CIA reverted to its old practices to fund its war on Nicaragua. Planes from the USA carrying arms and equipment for the *contras* on the southern front dropped their assignment in Costa Rica and flew on to Colombia. They returned packed with cocaine courtesy of the Medellin cartel. This was delivered to ranches in the north of the country belonging to one John Hull, a US citizen working closely with the CIA and the National Security Council in support of the Nicaraguan rebels. All of which was revealed when a government transport aircraft crashed near the ranch killing all seven occupants. Further information came out when pilots arrested on other drugs charges – Gerardo Duran, George Morales, Gary Wayne Betzner and

Pakia, Thailand: the Sae Yang family used to take opium. Now they are heroin addicts – Credit: Patrick Zachman/Magnum

Michael Tolliver – testified to a Senate committee (it sat from January 1986 to November 1998 and incontrovertibly established the CIA-drugs-arms-*contras* links) on their involvement in this particular traffic. Tolliver told the committee that in 1984 he had twice taken arms to the *contras* in Costa Rica and returned each time with half a tonne of

cocaine. He added that in March 1986 he had carried 15 tonnes of weapons for the *contras* to Agnacate airbase in Honduras and delivered in return 25,306 pounds of marijuana to the US airbase at Homestead. He was paid US$75,000 for the round trip.

Before the war in Afghanistan, opium was produced for long-term traditional users of the drug – chiefly the Ismaeli opium smokers of Badakhshan – and for its uses in medicine and foodstuffs; trafficking in the drug was illegal and fiercely repressed by the government. After the Russian invasion in December 1979, there was no central government capable of controlling the traffic. Persistent bombing of the poppy fields by the Russians and their Afghan allies reduced the farmers to smaller and smaller areas of cultivation – and drove them to find ways of maximising the income from their crop by converting it into heroin. At this point, the illegal trade remained largely in the hands of smugglers, the *mujahedin* contenting themselves with levying a tax as the merchandise crossed their territory. All this was about to change as the anti-communist/CIA/drug dealer troika got into the act and the Pakistani military set up hundreds of heroin-processing laboratories in the lawless tribal agencies on the borders of Pakistan and Afghanistan.

The USA decided to channel its substantial financial and military aid to the Afghan resistance exclusively through the Pakistan army's secret service, the Inter Services Intelligence (ISI). The latter used its monopoly to favour the most fundamentalist of the *mujahedin* groups – such as the Hezbi Islami of Gulbuddin Hekmatyar and those to which men like Osama Bin Laden belonged – and to secure an important stake in the heroin business. Even under the censorship of General Zia Ul Haq, the Pakistani press was reporting how sealed lorries of the National Logistic Cell were seen delivering arms to the *mujahedin* and returning from Afghanistan with the opium that would be transformed into heroin in labs under the control of the military in the tribal agencies. This in turn was exported to Europe via Iran and the notorious Balkan Highway. Between 1979 and 1989, the expanding traffic of these networks was responsible for the rise in opium production from around 400 tonnes to 1,500 tonnes a year.

And it was the ISI who reaped the lion's share of the profits in the decade of the Soviet occupation of Afghanistan. These it put to use in a variety of ways: covert operations in India via the Muslims of Kashmir and the Sikhs in the Punjab; equipment for the Pakistan army; even, say sources in European intelligence services, for the purchase of components for Pakistan's nuclear bomb, then still a closely guarded secret.

Accused by the USA of financing itself from the production and trade in drugs, the Taliban could rightly reply that it had done no more than take over the networks first developed by the CIA's protégés and later run by various *mujahedin* commanders.

In Asia, as in Latin America, US policy in the years of the Cold War proper and during the confrontation of the blocs, not only contradicted the country's claim to be the world leader in the war on drugs, but prevented it making certain strategic choices vital to US interests: to pursue the fight against Islamic terrorism, ensure nuclear non-proliferation and to ensure a lasting peace between India and Pakistan.

Since the fall of the Berlin Wall, practices that were more or less a monopoly of the secret services, have been 'democratised'. Drugs have become a nerve centre of regional wars in all the 'grey areas' of the world – Africa and Latin America as well as the former communist world. Local governments and power blocks, no longer supported by one or other of the superpowers, have turned to drugs to finance their wars, most of which have an ethnic, tribal, religious or nationalist colouring. But even here, the shadowy links between local protagonists and the agents of the USA persist. Since 1991, various Albanian networks have been trading heroin to buy light weapons. Switzerland, where weapons are on more or less open sale, has been an important centre for the traffic. The arms are taken to the majority Albanian areas of Macedonia bordering Kosovo. According to gun runners who have been arrested, particularly in Hungary, the arms were to support 'an uprising against the Serbs'. The emergence of the UCK (Kosovo Liberation Army) in 1997 was the culmination of this operation.

Meanwhile, as US instructors were 'advising' UCK troops [as they had done for the Taliban in the mosques and *madrasas* of Pakistan earlier in the decade, Ed.], the Italian police were denouncing the collaboration between the Albanian groups and the Italian mafia in arms for drugs deals. According to the Milan police, the biggest of the groups, between 50 and 60 strong, is that of Agim Gashi, a Kosovar Albanian who furnishes the heroin for *Ndrangheta* in Calabria and *Cosa Nostra* in Sicily. Another is led by Rivan Peshkepia, an Albanian with his own sources of supply in Turkey, who passes the heroin from the port of Durres in southern Albania to Bari in Montenegro by the Otranto Canal. He boasts of his friendship with Albania's previous president, Sali Berisha, and carries a diplomatic passport. At the beginning of February this year, an Albanian network smuggling heroin, cocaine and arms out of Durres on ships bound for Genoa and Trieste was broken up. The Albanians were trading heroin for cocaine with Nigerians in order to diversify their goods. According to members of the group, Croats were providing the weapons from former Yugoslav stocks.

The Albanian dealers preserve close links with their clan chiefs inside the country, whom they keep well supplied with a ready flow of cash. They also give financial support to the UCK, despite the fact that the latter, claims the Italian police, has its own drugs networks working on its behalf. According to an investigation carried out by the Italian magazine *Micromega*, Italian and Albanian godfathers are taking part in public demonstrations in support of the UCK and building contacts with prominent political figures in Italy. The US government has made no comment on their activities and no-one doubts that, as in the days of the Cold War, they will continue to be set down as profit and loss in the balance sheet of 'reasons of state'. ❏

Alain Labrousse is the director of Observatoire Geopolitique Des Drogues and the author of La drogue, l'argent et les armes *(Fayard, Paris 1991)*
Translated by Judith Vidal-Hall

CHRIS ELLISON

You say you want a revolution

In the last decade few things have had more impact on our lives than Information Technology – but does upheaval amount to revolution?

The collapse of the Berlin Wall marked the end of an era that began with the Bolshevik Revolution in 1917, almost a century ago. No sooner had the last remnants of the old Revolution been torn down, however, than a new revolution was announced: the Information Revolution. As early as 1991 US vice-president Al Gore was credited with championing it with the introduction of the phrase 'the information superhighway'. Since then the Information Revolution, its potential, its consequences, and its supposed risks have dominated debate and discussion for almost the entire decade.

The Information Revolution is not just associated with the development of the Internet but with all manner of Information Communication Technologies (ICTs) including mobile telecommunications, cable and satellite. More so than the Industrial Revolution, with which it is often compared, it continues to be seen by many not just as a technological transformation, but as a genuine social revolution set to change society radically.

Just as the *Communist Manifesto* ushered in the Bolshevik Revolution, so *UK Wired* saw fit to write its own *Wired Manifesto for the Digital Society*:

> 'The digital revolution that is sweeping the world is actually a communications revolution that is transforming society. When used by people and communities who understand it, digital technology allows information to be transmitted and transmuted

in fundamentally limitless ways. This ability is the basis of economic success around the world… It offers a new democracy dominated neither by the vested interests of political parties nor the mob's baying howl. It can narrow the gap that separates capital from labour; it can deepen the bonds between the people and the planet.'

Wired were certainly not alone in their belief in the onset of a communications transformation that would revolutionise society. In the following year, John Donovan's *The Second Industrial Revolution* put the Information Revolution on a par with the technological explosion that accompanied the advent of capitalism. Only last year Ira Magaziner, senior adviser to the US president, made a similar comparison: 'Just as the Industrial Revolution brought a change in our necessities, legally and commercially, so this Information Revolution will also bring changes.'

The development of ICTs is certainly set to transform the way in which the western world communicates with itself and with the rest of the planet. That change is likely to have a dramatic impact on the way in which people work and the jobs that they do. But does it honestly represent a social revolution?

Ironically, the Information Revolution has occurred at a time when the challenge to the existing social order, namely capitalist society and the market, is at an all time low. With the end of the Cold War, Margaret Thatcher's celebrated pro-market epithet of TINA: 'There Is No Alternative', has become a harsh political reality. As Lester Thurow describes in his analysis *The Future of Capitalism*: 'The market, and the market alone, rules. No one doubts it.' Contrary to the view expressed in *Wired*, there is less challenge to the gap between capital and labour than ever before. This lack of alternatives has expressed itself in electoral apathy. For example, this year's turnout for the UK's elections to the European Parliament was the lowest electoral turnout ever. As if to underline the fact that this was not simply an indication of people's attitude to Europe, a by-election in Leeds Central in the same week saw a turnout of less than 20% – the lowest in the UK since WWII.

Since real world democracy now seems elusive and sterile, some have turned to ICTs in the hope they will provide a positive alternative. One example is virtual democracy. The vision is that for the first time it might be practically possible to involve ordinary people in making day-to-day political decisions. Politics will cease to be dominated by the vested interests of political parties, just as the *Wired Manifesto* predicts. This involvement – goes the argument – will help to combat people's sense of isolation and apathy.

However, having one's say is not equal to democratic participation. The sad fact is that allowing people to express their opinions on things cannot compensate for the lack of ideas and the absence of a dynamic for social change in the real world.

There are those who hold out hope that cyberspace can offer an alternative society that will achieve many of the ideals that appear elusive in the offline world. In the early days of chat rooms, for example, many people suggested that discrimination was not possible since you could not see whether the person you were talking to was black or white, male or female. As the classic *New Yorker* cartoon captioned: 'On the Internet, nobody knows you're a dog.' Unfortunately for this thesis, one of the most popular opening questions for new visitors soon became 'Are you female?'

The Internet and particularly electronic commerce are also sometimes held up for their potential to liberate peoples of the developing world by allowing direct trade, thus eliminating loss in profit through multiple middlemen. But this freedom loses much of its significance when 60% of that world still lacks electricity, let alone telephones, modems and access to the Internet.

It is certainly true that the Internet has the potential for an increase in liberation through freedom of expression. But beyond that the Internet is being celebrated not for what it can add to the real world but as a social and ideological alternative to it. The truth is that information and communications technology can add nothing to a society that wields low expectations for what humanity can achieve offline.

Despite the over-reaching optimism with which some embrace ICTs, many people remain fairly cynical about technology and the potential for human intervention in the world.

As a consequence of the expansion of ICTs, society projects its anxieties and preoccupations onto them. There is nothing surprising in this – each new technological development is unerringly met with a fair dose of ambivalence and suspicion.

For the first time in human history, mass communication has ceased to be the preserve of the rich and powerful. The Internet allows ordinary people, armed with not much more than a modem and a computer, to communicate with millions of others around the globe in a matter of seconds. But rather than embrace this technology unequivocally for its liberating potential, the Internet has been met with suspicion, fear and condemnation. Focus has been on the negative aspects of the freedom of expression that the Internet affords. Most notable is the panic around the existence of pornography on the Net, in spite of the fact that BBC research indicated pornographic websites constitute less than 0.002% of all sites on the Net. Yet proposals to regulate and censor all Internet material continue.

Implicit in the focus on offensive material is the growing lack of faith in the ability of ordinary Internet users, the 'baying mob' as the *Wired Manifesto* refers the them, to form their own judgments about material. Thus sites which are deemed to express hatred or promote racism are frequently held up as justification for the need to censor the Internet. Few people question why it is assumed those Net users will spontaneously sympathise with the views that are expressed, nor why their removal should have any impact on changing any such existing sympathies. Internet users are crudely depicted as extremists, racists and pornographers or, at least, as innocent and vulnerable victims in need of protection by the more morally discriminating.

The Internet typifies post-Cold War society. The world, it seems, has rejected ideologies extolling collective action, or emphasising the progression or 'perfectibility' of mankind. With the collapse of major social movements, people are increasingly isolated and individualised. What more appropriate technology could there be than one such as the Internet which involves masses of people but brings them together as individuals?

In the absence of any real belief in the prospects for humanity in the offline world, the Information Revolution takes on a momentum of its own. Information technology is filling the vacuum left by the lack of political ideology in the real world. But rather than being a tool that could be manipulated to improve people's lives, there is a growing sense that it is the technology that controls people's lives. Our lack of faith in our ability to shape our destinies means that technologies such as the Internet become the focus of our hopes as well as our fears.

Scarcely a week goes by without the Internet being charged as an accessory to yet another crime or social disorder, from gun-toting teenagers to paedophile networks. Regulation is repeatedly demanded to protect people, usually children, and prevent the Information Revolution from getting out of control. Simultaneously, the Information Revolution is held up as the potential saviour of democracy: we hope it can resolve the crisis of apathy among the electorate.

But this has little to do with technology itself. Rather, it is a consequence of the demise of pre-Cold War attempts to create a positive future for humanity. ICTs are neither the cause of nor the solution to today's social problems. If we are determined to solve the latter, we must seek other remedies, ones that restore faith in humanity's ability to control its destiny and liberate its potential to do so. ❏

Chris Ellison (chris@netfreedom.org) is the founder of the cyber rights organisation Internet Freedom and a columnist for Practical Internet magazine. Additional research by Alan Docherty

SANTIAGO KOVADLOFF

Economic dictators

Globalisation, local rivalries and powerful neighbours in the north together ensure that instability and inequality remain endemic in Latin America

At least there's consensus on one thing: the fall of the Berlin Wall was also the fall of the last bastion of communist propaganda. The revolutionary maxim upholding equality among men, continually undermined even in the socialist world, is now being rolled back still further under the irresistible tide of uniformity imposed by globalisation. The banner held aloft in the belief that men are united by a common humanity has been torn down and one announcing that we are what we consume has been raised in its place.

By the time the Wall crumbled, the entire portfolio of Marxist ideals had already turned to dust in Latin America. Even Cuba was no more than a pathetic reliquary of its own past aspirations. From their outset, the 1980s were characterised by a continent-wide transition of the military regimes that had survived a generalised and merely formal restoration of democracy. The right-wing had put paid to leftist internationalism, and globalisation settled the matter by terminating the intrinsically weak claims of national sovereignty still advanced by the Right. In Latin America – and not only there – economic determinism assumed the dictatorial role formerly the remit of the authoritarian State. This in turn sharply accentuated the division between northern and southern hemispheres in terms of both efficiency and ethics. This division meant that wherever local democracies reappeared they were trapped in an internal contradiction: as their currencies strengthened so human life declined in value. The message was clear and irrefutable: whoever failed to consume would be consumed. This new order of the day advanced through the regional economies over and again at the cost of human suffering. It flourished wherever people were excluded and marginalised. There proved to be a poverty even worse than that in the existing slums and *favelas* inhabited by those the system had already rejected.

From the above, it is easy to draw the painful conclusion that at the close of the 20th century the major problems that have afflicted Latin America since the 19th persist unresolved. The emancipation we wrested from Spain and Portugal failed to bring to an end the sufferings of our southern hemisphere. In all essential respects we continue to resemble more a continental agglomerate than an organic assembly of nations. This rift between appearance and reality has been exploited by both local and overseas forces of globalisation. A new mask both covers and reveals the same old inequalities.

Beyond the sense of righteous indignation or melancholy nostalgia we can learn an invaluable lesson: for Latin America to 'integrate into the world', as the phrase goes, we must have something to contribute to the process, including a discussion of the values we may wish the world we are on the point of joining to uphold. If isolationism has always been sterile and is now a practical impossibility, an amorphous incorporation into the whole is no more than a way of projecting our familiar absence onto a wider screen.

Dehumanisation has its own geography: it renders us invisible to those who have no desire to acknowledge it. It has to be confronted once we ask ourselves specific questions as to the role and nature of Latin America's national cultures and the part that a responsible and openly democratic state should play in their development.

If we want to begin to examine the type of role that might be advisable for a nation state within the southern hemisphere, it's essential that we open with the warning that so far the function of the State has evolved from a form of centralised paternalism (Octavio Paz's 'philanthropic ogre') into an overwhelmingly managerial administration, primarily concerned with the privatisation of goods and services. Is there any way of escaping these alternatives? Yes, on the assumption that human suffering ceases to be a negotiable variable and the necessary price of economic stability; yes, once economic determinism evokes the same political indignation and resolution for change that the dysfunctional centralised state once provoked. Of course, for this to happen, humanity must be put at the centre of things and its existence valued at more than a percentage point in this or that calculation. For us to reach the stage where we are something more than a cipher in the ratings depends on a number of factors. But we ourselves are one of those factors.

To its shame, globalisation in Latin America does not promote co-operation but rather competition of the most savage variety. It serves to advance neither interdependence nor egalitarianism but rather new forms of dependence and the persistence of underdevelopment. This, obviously, has nothing to do with the assumedly inherent nature of globalisation but lies in the manner in which it is conceived and applied, in the various interests which stand to benefit from its implementation, and in the ineptitude shown by national cultures attempting to block the devouring capacity of globalisation to swallow all that stands in its way. As Jesus Maria Barbero writes: 'The rationale behind neo-liberal modernisation rejects social emancipation in favour of the logic of competitiveness where rules are no longer put in place by the State but by a market converted into the organising principle of society as a whole.'

The impact of globalisation on Latin American regional integration is radically different from its impact on, say, Europe. The countries of western Europe are achieving their integration at a regional and continental level after having consolidated their respective identities over a period of centuries; in addition, they have reinforced these identities within a deeply rooted and continuous democratic framework. By contrast, Latin American countries are still in search of both regional and continental harmonisation without having consolidated their individual national identities within an unequivocally democratic system. Is it really necessary to remind ourselves of the chronic instabilities of Colombia or Paraguay? The intermittent convulsions of Venezuela or Ecuador? The ambitions held by the presidents of Argentina and Peru for re-election?

The countries of Central and South America have set off in search of a greater interdependence without any guarantee of their internal autonomy and while still subject to crises of instability that can compromise not only their regional markets but also the confidence of their principal trading partners.

Given its subordination to private interests bent on securing further quick and juicy profits, Latin American integration will continue to do violence to existing enfeebled regional and national identities. As a

result, uniformity is gaining ground at the expense of diversity and individuality, above all at the expense of the right to dignity in the lives of those most in need of it.

Globalisation, implemented according to totalitarian criteria, promotes cultural fragmentation and the substitution of stereotyping for real experience, the rhetoric of identity for genuine discussion. Within globalisation as currently practised, the desire to submerge all differentiation in order to secure its own survival through the primacy of sectoral over collective interests, of egotism over solidarity, of technocracy over the ethical foundations of knowledge is paramount. How remote the days when the Marxist left was accused of reducing everything to a single economic dimension now appear. The Wall has fallen; what has not crumbled is economic determinism. On the contrary, its powers have been magnified and it is stronger than ever. ❏

Santiago Kovadloff is an Argentine writer living in Buenos Aires. His books include A Catacomb Culture *(1982) and* The Primordial Silence *(1993). Translated by Amanda Hopkinson*

Radio Free Maine

Noam Chomsky, Camille Paglia, Howard Zinn, Cornel West and Edward Said in your living room?

Radio Free Maine

brings a wealth of dissenting voices into your home, putting you at the heart of the debate.
Radio Free Maine recordings are available on both audio and video cassette. For a full catalogue and price listing contact:
Roger Leisner at

Radio Free Maine

PO Box 2705, Augusta, Maine 04338
Tel/Fax: (207)622 6629 or on the web at
WWW.RADIOFREEMAINE.COM

CHRISTA WOLF

Style censor

'How is someone to write without the censorship to which he has always been subjected?' asked Heinrich Heine in the Paris of 1848. 'Style, decency and grammatical structure will become obsolete. If ever I were to write badly, I would think well, let the censor alter or delete it. I could always depend on censorship. Yet now I feel quite helpless! I still hope it is not true; that censorship will prevail.'

I wonder whether some of our colleagues will themselves soon hear Heine's self-mocking fears as the voice of nostalgia; if they have not already done so. I should like to warn against this, and against the suppression of such nostalgia as is being done through the probing inspection of mistakes on to which a sense of retrogressive melancholy clings. These days, I would much rather hear colleagues testify to the joys of familiar censorship than be told of their suffering under it. I wish that the board of this organisation [the Writers' Union of the GDR] had defended itself against the criticism, open and implicit, that has been levelled against it and the function it performed under the old regime. Had this been the case, the question of these functions could have been examined as part of the wider debate. In my opinion, pointing the finger of blame at individuals in cases where many were involved achieves nothing. What is important is that we create an atmosphere in which we can learn and express the need for reconciliation and its benefits. We must all shoulder responsibility, not simply project that responsibility on to others.

The Writers Union is facing difficult times; its situation mirrors that of the country in general. It must take a long look at itself, but avoid the self-destructive tendencies that have been widespread these past weeks. An individual can do this through change; an organisation must start afresh. We have spent too much time drafting new statutes. I do not wish to undermine this work, especially after all we have experienced in the realm of laws and decrees that acted as the instruments of censorship and other sorts of oppression. Extensive debate on rules and regulations leaves less room for debate on the other things we had hoped to talk about, and that the public demands we address.

What we must all realise is that this is no longer a political organisation that may speak on cultural and political issues. And although we must learn to accept this, we are retreating perhaps a little too far. Like many people in this country, authors are finding themselves facing financial difficulties. The basis for their material well-being – publishing companies – are under threat. The Writers Union must address urgently the hardship facing its members.

It seems to me that many delegates here are concerned about the lack of any weighty argument over the past few days. This mood has manifested itself in criticism of me because, for example, I do not intend to stand for election to the board of this union, and I would like to take the opportunity to respond to some questions and allegations.

Many may remember that I have worked for many years on various committees, including the executive committee of the Writers Union. The union was given the task of creating an identity for young people. In local branches, writers who were critical of the government ignited debate and were able to protect their colleagues from official censure. There was an atmosphere of friendship and solidarity. The events surrounding the poet Wolf Bierman's expatriation in 1976, 'for criticising the regime', polarised writers in East Germany. This polarisation has merely faded into the background and remains unresolved. The dismissal at the behest of the authorities of fellow members soured my relationship with the union. The leadership at the time did nothing about the dismissals. I realised then that it was impossible to be anything more that a half-hearted proof-reader of union procedure.

We have reached the end of that stage where, as writers, we were asked to represent others. No other institution could have produced the type of criticism that has torn this country apart and it was far more risky for others to speak out than it was for us. Meanwhile, in the West German media there is a deliberate and concentrated plan afoot (in the East German media too during this frenzied election campaign). Its aim is to propagate the idea that East German literature and its authors are now as obsolete as the German Democratic Republic. I am not troubled by critical, outspoken, humanist, daring literature. It is linked to this country and to the conflicts we bore and which have defined us. To deny these roots would stifle creativity at source. The reformed Writers Union must be mindful that what is required in these difficult times is solidarity.

For solidarity is the key word in the new relationship with our readers. We no longer need to represent their interests since many of them have learned to speak for themselves. We must show them our own weaknesses, that we are helpless, make mistakes and are imperfect. We must ask them to show leniency and to help us. We would like to know what they expect from us now that many of us find ourselves with the difficult task of redefining new roles in society.

Whatever may come – new social framework and economic reform, challenges, temptations, and defamation, new possibilities and opportunities – we belong to a rare and privileged group of German writers that has lived through and participated in the disintegration of part of Germany and the ensuing process of revolutionary renewal. We form the dissenting voice that questions future developments and we must find the energy to resist any impending restoration of old ideas. This sets us apart from other areas of society but ultimately it will enable us to establish closer links with a new readership.

During the re-establishment of Prussian rule in Berlin, the writer Bettine von Arnim, in a display of persistence and nerve, arranged posts at the university for two lecturers who had been expelled from the University of Göttingen for insubordination. They were Jakob and Wilhelm, the Brothers Grimm. Even that fine bureaucratic line that delineated German states in the 19th century could be manipulated. Should we now collectively lose our head, give up our history, our courage, our self-confidence and our much tested experience of dissent simply because the ruling powers that we oppose have changed? ❏

Christa Wolf is a novelist and critic. This is excerpted from a speech given to the Writers Union of the GDR on 3 March 1990
Translated by Syra Morley

Striking the Gong

This Saturday a small group of Londoners will gather in Hyde Park, whose Speakers' Corner is still a byword for free speech in these parts. Behind the bandstand, they will practise five exercises designed to 'relieve their bodies of bad elements', cultivate their *falun* and stimulate their *xinxing*, according to traditional Chinese holistic teaching – and China's newest *bête noire*, Li Hongzhi. In April, some 10,000 followers of Li's fitness regime, *Falun Gong,* shocked President Jiang Zhemin when they gathered outside the leadership compound in Beijing to politely, but insistently, request official recognition of their school of exercise. These were not the radical students who had tried in Tiananmen Square to stampede the masses into sweeping away the dictatorship of the Party 10 years earlier. They were middle-aged housewives, bank clerks and teachers, the salt of the new Chinese high-rises. More worrying still, by official accounts, some 30,000 party cadres in Beijing alone had joined the movement. It claims to have 100 million adherents; 2 million is probably closer to the mark.

With the Tiananmen anniversary safely out of the way, Jiang felt free to act. In the early hours of 20 July police and security units rounded up *Falun Gong* co-ordinators in Harbin, Jinzhou and Dalian Cities, causing protests in 30 other cities the next day. Though the demonstrators, true to their beliefs, offered no resistance, heads were smashed. On 22 July the ministry of civil affairs officially outlawed *Falun Gong*, denouncing the organisation as 'an evil cult ... advocating superstition, spreading fallacies and jeopardising social stability.' Li Hongzhi, it affirmed, was 'not the Highest Buddha', merely a dangerous huckster.

There followed scenes reminiscent of the Cultural Revolution as thousands of *Falun Gong* practitioners were herded into football stadia, agricultural institutes and schools until they recanted. As with other campaigns against dissident thought, there were televised 'confessions of error', re-education sessions and pressure to eliminate *Falun Gong* through threats to work, education, pensions and housing (p81).

A US$6,000 reward was posted for information leading to the arrest of Li Hongzhi, 'a male, ethnic Han, speaking Mandarin with a north-eastern accent', according to the official description. Ironically for a man whose status in Beijing now matches that of Osama bin Ladin in Washington DC, Li had moved to the New York borough of Queens a year earlier 'because his daughter wanted a US high school education'. Most of his time is spent cultivating his *falun* – though he sometimes helps Mrs Li with the groceries.

There is much to marvel at in this Borgesian episode in which a keep-fit regime, not wildly dissimilar to the *Tai Chi* promoted to the masses throughout the Mao era, is abruptly criminalised and its followers hunted down like the devil's spawn. China is notoriously intolerant of organised worship, permitting only a handful of established religions, all answerable to the Party. But while mingling different elements of Buddhism, Taoism and Confucianism in his recipe for wholesome living, Li denies any supernatural powers. *Falun Gong,* said his spokesman, 'is a national pastime. Can you imagine the reaction if the US banned baseball?'

But there is more to *Falun Gong* than meets the eye. The reticence, which hitherto characterised its adherents, is a surer guarantor of survival in the brutal shadow theatre of Beijing politics than the overt challenge raised in Tiananmen Square in 1989. 'Gongists' vastly outnumber Chinese democrats. Their commitment to the core values of 'Truth, Compassion and Forbearance', moreover, contains a coded reproof to the corruption that permeates ruling circles and that has worsened since their adoption of that other product of the west, rampant capitalism.

Far more than democracy, *Falun Gong* is fundamentally a Chinese phenomenon and a reminder that, when the voice of dialectical materialism begins to waver, China reverts to the babble of its dialects. In search of an historical precedent, it is perhaps more useful to go back to 1851 when the Protestant convert Hung Xiu-Quan amassed a vast army of religious acolytes and founded the Taiping Heavenly Kingdom. After 13 bloody years, the Qing dynasty was only saved through western intervention. As the People's Republic nears its 50th birthday, Beijing may have found the parallel eery.

But it may be comforting to remember, when placidly stimulating one's *xinxing*, that of the five exercises needed to cultivate the *falun*, the two most important involve nothing more strenuous than sitting still.
And waiting. ❏

Michael Griffin

A censorship chronicle incorporating information from the American Association for the Advancement of Science Human Rights Action Network (AAASHRAN), Amnesty International (AI), Article 19 (A19), the BBC Monitoring Service Summary of World Broadcasts (SWB), the Committee to Protect Journalists (CPJ), Canadian Journalists for Free Expression (CJFE), Glasnost Defence Foundation (GDF), The UN's Integrated Regional Information Network (IRIN), the Inter-American Press Association (IAPA), the International Federation of Journalists (IFJ/FIP), the International Federation of Newspaper Publishers (FIEJ), Human Rights Watch (HRW), the Media Institute of Southern Africa (MISA), International PEN (PEN), Open Media Research Institute (OMRI), Radio Free Europe/Radio Liberty (RFE/RL), Reporters Sans Frontières (RSF), the World Association of Community Broadcasters (AMARC), World Association of Newspapers (WAN), the World Organisation Against Torture (OMCT), Writers in Prison Committee (WiPC) and other sources

AMERICAN SAMOA

On 14 June the *Samoa News* accused government adviser Gus Hanneman of slapping *Samoa News* journalist **Fili Sagapolutele** in the face in the hallway of the legislative building. Sagapolutele had used government records to report on Hanneman's annual salary and recent pay increase. *Samoa News* editor Scott McPhee said that the paper would continue to report on salaries of public officials. 'The public has the right to know how every penny of their money is being spent and reporters have every right to pursue that cause,' he said. (Pacific Islands News Association)

ANGOLA

Information Minister Pedro Hendrik Vaal Neto said during a 1 June press conference that the government was contemplating 'resorting to violence' against independent media which do not support the war against UNITA [National Union for the Total Independence of Angola]. He further accused certain media of being the 'fifth column of Jonas Savimbi's rebel movement'. (RSF)

Journalist **Gustavo Costa** claimed in June that he had been placed under 'physical and psychological pressure' to reveal his sources following an article on corruption within President Dos Santos' inner circle, published in Portugal's *Expresso* magazine in April. (*Index* 4/1999). (Media Institute of Southern Africa)

On 9 August the chief editor of the Catholic FM station Radio Ecclesia, **Paulo Juliao**, and two other journalists, **Laurinda Tavares** and **Filipe Joaquim**, were detained by plain-clothes officers of the Criminal Investigation Department (DNIC) after the station re-broadcast a BBC interview with UNITA leader Jonas Savimbi, which was also aired by state television service TPA. Tavares and Joaquim were interrogated for four hours at the DNIC and released by midnight. On 10 August, Juliao was rearrested along with station director **Emanuel da Mata** after the station again broadcast the interview during its noon bulletin. (Media Institute of Southern Africa)

ARGENTINA

Pedro Scarano, director of the publications *Bajando Noticias* and *Identidad Virtual*, and his family, continued to suffer harassment in early July. Scarano received threatening phone calls, had his personal telephone lines tapped and was followed by unidentified individuals. Since March 1996 the journalist has been subjected to six attacks and 40 threats. (*Periodistas*)

On 31 July the hotel room of the daily *Pagina/12* journalist **Cristian Alarcon** was broken into and some information stolen. The following day a van followed him at high speed as he was heading towards the airport. He had recently received two warnings advising him to stop investigating the confrontation between a group of unemployed persons and former members of the intelligence services. (*Periodistas*)

AZERBAIJAN

Parliamentary deputy Jalal Aliyev, brother of the president, sued *Bakinski Bulvar* journalist **Irada Husseinova** for libel and defamation on 18 June. The suit relates to a December 1998 article on the Azeri Fuel Filling Service that described Aliyev as the 'King of the Oil Industry'. If found guilty, Husseinova faces up to five years' imprisonment. (GDF, International Helsinki Federation for Human Rights)

Elman Maliyev, a crime correspondent with *Hurriyet* newspaper, was beaten by two unknown assailants on 19 June. When, during the beating, Maliyev threatened to call police the assailants replied that they were police. The incident is now being investigated by Narimanov district police. (GDF, RSF)

During a 25 June debate on the proposed media law, parliamentarians accused the media of 'immorality', 'betrayal', and 'seeking to undermine Azerbaijan's statehood'. Jalal Aliyev took the opportunity to describe male journalists as 'rogues' and their female colleagues as 'whores'. On 1 July, US Ambassador to Azerbaijan Stanley Escudero said that, if adopted, the law would negate the 1998 decision to abolish censorship. (RFE/RL)

Ten youths forced their way into the editorial offices of *Hurriyet* newspaper on the evening of 29 June and beat up four journalists. The assailants linked the beating to the paper's coverage of an 'oil mafia' in Gyanja. (RFE/RL)

On 30 June three men claiming to work for the National Security Ministry pulled *Yeni Musavat* correspondent **Kamil Tagisoy** from a car and took him for interrogation about his sources of information on President Heidar Aliyev's health. Tagisoy was badly beaten, stripped and photographed naked by the men, who threatened him and editor **Rauf Arifoglu** with death if they continued their investigations. Tagisoy had been singled out for

criticism during Jalal Aliyev's diatribe against journalists, five days earlier. The next day, President Aliyev ordered an investigation into the beating. (GDF, RFE/RL)

In early July, Parliament Speaker Murtuz Alaskarov launched a case against the editor of the newspaper *Sharg* and journalist **Vefa Allahverdieva** for 'insulting his honour and dignity' in an article in the newspaper's 3-6 June issue. Alaskarov is demanding 50 million manats (US$12,500) in compensation. The newspaper was convicted of the offence on 31 July and fined an unknown amount. (*Turkistan Newsletter*, RFE/RL)

Police attempted to prevent a 9 July protest by more than 70 journalists against State interference and intimidation. During the protest, outside the state-owned Azerbaijan publishing house, plain-clothes officers detained **Shakhin Jafarly** of *Yeni Musavat* and **Javid Jabbaroglu** of *Hurriyet*. After one hour's detention at a nearby police station both were released. (GDF)

Journalist **Fuad Gakhramanly**, sentenced in November 1998 to 18 months' imprisonment (*Index* 1/1999, 4/1999) for writing an article that was never published, was one of 91 people pardoned by President Heidar Aliyev on 10 July. (RFE/RL)

Mirjavid Rahim, a reporter with the Baku daily newspaper *Uch Noqte*, was assaulted by three unidentified men outside the Supreme Court building, where he was covering the

high-profile trial of Bashir Hajiyev. Hajiyev is accused of embezzling 100 billion manats (US$40 million) from Russia's Prominvestbank, whose local branch he headed. (CPJ)

Recent publications: *Guide to Azerbaijan's Mass Media* (in Russian and English, contact ozulfugarov@osi-az.org)

BAHRAIN

On 8 July **Sheikh al-Jamri** (*Index* 3/1995, 4/1995, 6/1995, 2/1996, 3/1999, 4/1999) was unexpectedly pardoned and released from a 10-year prison sentence and a US$15 million fine which had been imposed by a court the previous day. The writer, poet, judge and member of the now-dissolved parliament had been detained for three years prior to trial. Security forces have prevented journalists from entering the Bani Jamra area where Al-Jamri resides. (WiPC, PEN, Bahrain Freedom Movement)

BANGLADESH

On 1 July sculptor **Shamin Sikder** received death threats from religious extremists claiming to be members of the local Taliban movement. In a letter signed by the commander of the Taliban Bahini, Sikder, an associate professor of the Dhaka University Department of Sculpture and the Institute of the Fine Arts, was told she would be 'tortured to death' if she continued her work. The threat is believed to have been prompted by her sculpture depicting important events in the country's political history. (Media Watch)

On 27 July a mass grave, apparently from the 1971 liberation war, was discovered by workers extending a mosque in Dhaka's Mirpur district, close to an alleged site of massacres committed by the Pakistani military and their collaborators. Once forensic investigations are completed in Dhaka, London and New York, the Liberation Museum intends to file a case in either the International Court of Justice in The Hague or the UN Human Rights. (Agence France-Presse)

The government has banned the importation, distribution and sale of **Taslima Nasrin**'s *My Childhood*, it was reported on 13 August, because of what it termed the 'adverse effects' and the 'hurt' it might cause to religious sentiments. This is the second ban this year on her writing (*Index* 10/1993, 3/1994, 4/1994, 5/1994, 6/1994, 1/1995, 2/1995, 6/1996, 2/1997, 6/1998, 1/1999). (BBC)

BELARUS

Editor-in-chief of the independent weekly *Imya*, **Irina Khalip**, was detained in Minsk on 21 July by seven militia officers when she brought **Vyacheslav Sivchik**, one of the leaders of the People's Front of Belarus (PFB), to the main PFB building. She was taken to the offices of the Traffic Police, where she remained in custody for an hour before being released. The following morning, 22 July, five militia officers arrived at the offices of *Imya* with a warrant for her arrest issued by the prosecutor's office. The men also tried to

search the offices of the *Belorusskaya Gazeta*, which shares a floor with *Imya*. Journalists refused to let them in. A correspondent with the weekly *Belorusskaya Gazeta*, **Yegor Mayorchik**, also received a summons from the prosecutor's office over the publication of a story investigating the disappearance of the former interior minister, Yuri Zakharenko (*Index* 4/1999). (GDF, Belarus Association of Journalists)

On 26 July a Minsk Court ordered the independent newspaper *Belorusskaya Delovaya Gazeta* to pay 2.1 billion roubles (US$7,900) to Judge Nadzeya Chmara in compensation for 'moral damages' allegedly inflicted on her by the newspaper. The court also ordered staff reporter **Viktor Martynovych** to pay Judge Chmara 100 million roubles (US$500) in damages for his 'biased coverage' of the political corruption trial of Vasil Starovoytau, the former Central Bank director, over which she presided. (CPJ)

BELGIUM

On 13 July Belgian public prosecutor **Hubert Massa**, who headed inquires into the Marc Dutroux child abuse and murder case, committed suicide. Investigations into the Dutroux case have been characterised by blunders within the justice system and the police force. *(Daily Telegraph)*

BURKINA FASO

On 2 July security minister Djubrill Bassolé refused to allow

Reporters Sans Frontières to pursue a follow-up inquiry into the the death of editor **Norbert Zongo** in December 1998 (*Index* 2/1999). The minister claimed that its proposed visit to Ouagadougou was 'ill-timed' and could 'compromise the tranquillity' of the country, adding 'it would be preferable to postpone [the] mission to a more appropriate time, which would not hamper the investigation of the case'. (RSF)

CAMBODIA

Following last December's demonstrations against the proposed dumping of 3,000 tonnes of toxic waste near the port of Sihanoukville, charges against the 10 people arrested were dismissed by the judge on 22 July for lack of evidence. Of those arrested **Kim Sen** and **Meas Minear** from the Cambodian human rights organisation Licadho had been charged with robbery. The prosecution failed to produce any evidence or provide a single witness to support the charges. *(Financial Times)*

CAMEROON

On 16 July the editor-in-chief of *Le Serment*, **Anselme Mballa**, was sentenced to six months' imprisonment for defamation. He is accused of publishing an article critical of the behaviour of the state secretary for the post and telecommunications towards traditional chiefs. (RSF)

Journalist **Christophe Bobiokono** of the biweekly newspaper *Mutations* was arrested in Yaoundé and sentenced to a prison term on 22 July. Three days earlier the paper had published an article stating that the son of the minister for the economy and finance was granted public contracts on a regular basis. (RSF)

On 16 June, a letter bomb exploded at Edmonton's A-Channel Television newsroom, injuring assignment editor **Garnet Lewis** and reporter **Stacey Brotzel**. No motive has been uncovered as yet, but police are investigating a possible connection between this incident and two letter bombs sent to Edmonton and Calgary's police chiefs earlier this year. (CJFE, Reuters)

A Chechen correspondent for the Russian ITAR-TASS news agency, abducted by unknown assailants on 28 March after they broke into his flat in Grozny, was freed by his kidnappers on 19 June. **Said Isayev** was released in 'good condition' and without any payment of ransom. (CPJ)

Beijing police detained 11 Hong Kong-based journalists on 14 June as they were covering a visit by delegates from the territory's Federation of Students. The delegation was presenting a petition before the National People's Congress challenging China's authority to reinterpret the Basic Law, Hong Kong's 'mini-constitution'. The journalists were intercepted immediately on their arrival and detained for over an hour, during which time their videotapes were seized and they were warned not to report in the Tiananmen Square area without permission. Two journalists were detained separately and threatened with punishment if they reported on the group's detention. Meanwhile, Public Security Bureau officials prevented the student delegation from holding a press conference at their Beijing hotel, informing them that 'media coverage of [the petition] was illegal'. The petition challenged the Hong Kong government's request to the Congress for re-interpretation of the Right of Abode, following a Court of Appeal ruling that the government's expulsion of residents' children born on the mainland was unlawful. The Court's ruling has since been overturned, raising doubts about the Chinese government's promise of 'one country, two systems with a high degree of autonomy'. (Agence France-Presse, CPJ, Hong Kong Journalists Association)

State-run Xinhua news agency reported a 'warm welcome' on 18 June upon the arrival in Lhasa of Gyaincain Norbu, the boy chosen by Beijing as the reincarnation of the Panchen Lama, Tibetan Buddhism's second most powerful figure. Xinhua's account of 'deafening trumpets and drums' was ridiculed by the Tibetan government in exile, whose spokesperson said that 'if there is no fear of the gun, nobody would go'. Most Tibetans honour **Gedhun Choeki Nyima** – the boy chosen by the Dalai Lama as the true Panchen Lama – who disappeared soon after he was identified in 1995. Many Tibetans are reported to worship pictures of Gedhun in secret, despite Beijing's campaign to discredit the boy. (*Guardian*)

The authorities have continued to crack down on the banned China Democratic Party (CDP) in the wake of the Tiananmen Square anniversary. On 6 July CDP member **He Depu** was arrested by Beijing police without being formally charged and, the following day, **Liu Xianbin**, a core member of the party, was detained. On 2 August two members of the Beijing-Tianjin branch of the CDP, arrested on 29 June, were sentenced to lengthy jail sentences for 'subverting State power'. **Gao Hongming**, a former Beijing official who served a two-year sentence after the 1989 protests, was jailed for eight years **and Zha Jianguo**, a magazine publisher, received a nine-year sentence. Foreign reporters were prevented from attending the hearing. It is reported that **Xu Wenli**, who was sentenced to 13 years' imprisonment in December for his part in setting up the CDP, is seriously ill from bad prison conditions and beatings. **Han Lifa**, a CDP co-founder due to be released on 22 July, was given an extra two-year sentence on 29 July for going on hunger strike in protest against prison beatings. On 4 August **She Wanbao**, of the Sichuan branch of the CDP, was sentenced to 12 years for subversion. The Information Centre of Human Rights and Democratic

● ●

ALEJANDRA MATUS
First Anniversary

On 29 December 1973 13 ministers from the new government of General Augusto Pinochet joined senior members of Chile's High Court to celebrate the court's 150 anniversary in the palace of justice. On 1 March 1974 virtually the same cast congregated once more to listen to the inaugural discourse of the judicial year. It was a Friday. The country was still in a state of siege. The detention of members of the opposition had been massive and now word-of-mouth news about disappearances was more and more urgent

On the second floor of the palace of justice the military *junta's* first minister of justice Gonzalo Prieto, his under-secretary, Max Silva, the president of the College of Lawyers, Alejandro Silva Bascuñán, the president of the Court of Appeals of Santiago, José Cánovas and all the magistrates in charge were meeting their special guest, Helmut Kovold, president of the High Court of Hanover.

In the plenary room, Urrutia Manzano read his discourse. It was published the following day by *El Mercurio* newspaper under the headline 'Supreme Court president talks tough'. He told the company: 'After the events of the 11 December 1973, to which I shall refer later, I can emphatically assure you that the courts under our jurisdiction have acted according to the rule of law, that the administrative authority that rules Chile has followed our resolutions and that we respect our judges as they deserve. It gives me enormous pleasure to be able to say this.'

His memory of the Marxist government of Salvador Allende was still strong: such a government 'had lost the legitimacy it had obtained through its election to the National Congress as a result of its constant mistakes and open and repeated violation of the rule of law, both in letter and in spirit'.

He defended the new regime against the accusations of human rights violations, recalling what happened on 6 August 1970, before Allende took power. A group of lawyers had asked the Supreme Court to take measures to avoid the abuse and maltreatment of those under interrogation in police buildings and prisons. The court had investigated the accusations and, in less than 20 days, taken a good number of depositions. Nevertheless, Manzano said,

● ●

most of the complainants had been appointed to high positions in the Allende government and subsequently forgot all about their legal proceedings.

What was currently happening in Chile, he said, was not as serious as some had claimed: 'The majority of detainees who were so critical of the legal instruments which legalised the state of siege have been set free. Others are being tried in ordinary or military tribunals. As for those who are still detained under the emergency legislation of the state of siege, we are seeking to ensure their wellbeing and to establish, as soon as possible, the extent of their involvement in illegal activities. We hope to end their families' distress as soon as possible.'

The president of the High Court also noted that he had received a visit from two delegates of Amnesty International. They had expressed concern at the judiciary's indifference to international criticism of the violation of human rights in Chile. In particular, they were alarmed by the High Court's decision to abrogate its power of legal constraint over the War Council, which had ordered the execution of so many people.

Urrutia Manzon told his audience that he had explained to the delegates how 'exaggerated' their concerns were. Where executions had taken place, they were justified under the current legal framework in Chile and were in 'full harmony' with Chile's international commitments on human rights. The minister regretted that the Amnesty report had not includes his opinions: 'They prefer to believe anonymous rumours or vested interests,' he said, adding that 'human rights are respected in our motherland.' ❏

From Chapter IV of **Alejandra Matus***' Black Book of Chilean Justice (Planeta), the entire print run of which was seized by police on 14 April, on the instruction of the Santiago High Court, and subsequently banned. Matus, a journalist based in Miami, was awarded last year's Ortega y Gasset prize by Spain's El Pais for an article on the assassination of Orlando Letelier in Washington DC in 1976. The Black Book of Chilean Justice, a product of six years work, examines the conduct of the Chilean High Court since its inception 172 years ago but devotes half its content to the 16-year Pinochet regime.*

Movement in China reports that at least eight CDP activists have been jailed for attempting to subvert State power since May. (Reuters)

The editor of the *South China Morning Post* was replaced on 2 August after four years in charge of Hong Kong's leading English-language newspaper. **Jonathan Fenby**'s contract was not renewed and he has speculated that the owners are looking for someone with whom they feel 'more comfortable'. The *Post*, whose principal owner is one of Asia's richest men with good connections in Beijing, had taken a strong line against the Hong Kong government's decision to refer to Beijing for reinterpretation of the Territory's Right of Abode. A senior Chinese official recently told a group of Hong Kong journalists that some newspapers had 'fuelled the row' over the decision, although he didn't mention the *Post* by name. (*Guardian*)

Recent publications: *A Tradition of Intellectual Dissent: Tibetan Political Prisoners in Qinghai Province, Tibet Information Network Special Report, July 1999, ISSN 1355-3313)*

COLOMBIA

On 5 May President Andres Pastrana promised to pursue and broaden the investigations into the murder of journalists and to protect those who have been threatened. Since 1995, journalists have suffered increasing attacks, and according to the Foundation for the Freedom of the Press, 120 have been killed in the past 20 years.

On 30 June **Carlos Pulgarin**, a correspondent with the Monteria-based *El Tiempo*, left the region to protect his family after finding death threats on his answering machine. He was threatened after writing a report on the armed confrontation between the army, the Revolutionary Armed Forces (FARC), and paramilitary groups. (CPJ)

Also in June, reporter **Juan Carlos Aguiar** and cameraman **Jhon Jader Jaramillo** fled the country following death threats by telephone and in person. On 8 June they distributed images of the Chinchina lynching of shoemaker Jorge Delio Cardona. (Instituto de Prensa y Sociedad, Agencia de Noticias Nueva Colombia).

On 13 August the radio journalist and popular comedian **Jaime Garzón** was shot dead by two men on a motorcycle while driving to work. Garzón's biting satire and political parodies were broadcast on Radionet and a Caracol network television news program. He had been frequently threatened by Carlos Castaño, the leader of the United Self Defence Forces of Colombia (AUC), a right-wing paramilitary organisation that is fighting against leftist guerrillas. Garzón's colleagues said that the journalist had planned a meeting with Castaño for 14 August. Many believe that Castaño ordered the murder, either because of Garzón's journalistic work, or because of his contact with the guerrillas. Garzón served on a commission that was mediating between the National Liberation Army (ELN) and the

government, and regularly negotiated for the release of victims of guerrilla kidnappings. The AUC denies any responsibility in the murder. (CPJ)

COMOROS ISLANDS

Radio Ushababi, a pro-federation station on the breakaway island of Anjouan, ceased broadcasting on 9 August after a series of threats and attacks by separatist militiamen. The radio station was created on 1 June in Mutsamudu by a group of journalists opposed to the island's declaration of independence from the Islamic Republic of the Comoros in 1997. In 1997, the same group of young journalists was forced to cease publishing the newspaper *Ushababi*, following similar pressure against them. (RSF)

COTE D'IVOIRE

Police officers seized copies of the fifth issue of the monthly *Africa Golfe Eco* on 27 July. Copies of the paper, which specialises in economic issues, were taken from kiosks in Abidjan by security forces without a warrant. The issue contained a feature entitled 'Disinformation, manipulation, corruption, embezzlement, is the Bédié System at death's door?' (RSF)

CROATIA

On 7 June the editor-in-chief of the independent weekly *Nacional,* **Ivo Pukanic,** and **Robert Bajrusi**, a reporter on the same newspaper, were summoned by police and interrogated about an article claiming referees had been forced into favouring local football team Croatia in their championship-winning season. According to the report, the secret-service agency SZUP, under the orders of President Franjo Tudjman, had coerced referees and wiretapped sports officials and journalists. *Nacional* printed allegedly authentic SZUP documents to support their claims and, following searches of the offices of *Nacional* as well as the homes of Pukanic and Bajrusi, the police included the home of a former justice minister. The ministry of internal affairs has since approached the prosecutor general's office with the request to launch criminal cases Pukanic for 'printing State secrets'. (CPJ, *Observer*)

CZECHOSLOVAKIA

On 15 June a group of Roma children in the city of Ostrava, aided by local counsel and the European Roma Rights Centre, filed legal complaints after they were segregated into special schools for the mentally deficient on the basis of ethnicity. Roma pupils outnumber non-Roma by more than 27 to one, while approximately 75% of all Roma children in the state attend special schools. (European Roma Rights Centre)

DEMOCRATIC REPUBLIC OF CONGO

Jean-Fidèle Mamba was detained at the Penitentiary and Re-education Centre of Kinshasa on 20 May for having

penned two articles in *La Manchette*, entitled 'Kabila at bay' and 'Kabila angry with Kakudji'. On 27 May, **Loseke Lisumbu**, editor-in-chief of the *daily La Libre Afrique*, was arrested and accused of 'slander' for publishing an article: 'General discontent at the National Police' in the 25 May edition (*Index* 2/1999). The article stated that the National Police inspector-general had placed his sons in important leadership positions, rather than individuals considered 'better qualified'. (RSF)

In mid-July rebels seized the Maendeleo radio station's equipment. The station broadcasts in Bukavu region in the east, an area controlled by the Rwandan-backed rebels. (RSF)

In mid-July the minister of information and tourism, Didier Mumengi, banned the rebroadcast of all foreign programmes. (RSF)

On 26 July journalists **Jean Marie Kashila**, from the Congolese Press Agency, and **Bienvenu Tshiela**, with Kasai Horizon Radio-Television, were flogged by police officers in Mbuji-Mayi on the orders of the vice-governor of Kasai, Kalala Kaniki, who had accused the men of criticising him in their articles. (RSF)

On 9 August two independent dailies, *Le Phare* and *Le Potentiel*, published reports on a public hearing of the Military Court, during which the accused made mention of conspiracies within security services. On 11 August agents of the State Security

Council visited the two newspapers' offices to detain the authors of the reports, **Nounou Booto** of *Le Potentiel*, and **Fidèle Musangu** of *Le Phare*. Because the journalists were not there, the security services agents arrested the editor-in-chief of *Le Potentiel*, **Modeste Mutinga** (*Index* 3/1999). He was released the same evening. (RSF, CPJ)

EGYPT

On 27 May the People's Assembly finally passed Law 153/99, despite vociferous opposition from human rights groups and non-governmental organisations. The new law places NGOs under strict official control and provides the government with extensive powers over their management. (*Cairo Times*)

On 6 June **Gamal Fahamy** was sacked from the weekly *Al-Arabi* on the orders of the state-owned media agency Ahram, which prints and distributes *Al-Arabi*. In recent years Fahamy has been forced to move from one newspaper to another in search of space for his opposition views, while suffering imprisonment in the process. (*Index* 3/1998, 4/1998, /6/1998). (*Cairo Times*)

On 19 June a criminal court sentenced the head of the alternative journalists' union, **Hussein Al Matani,** to three and a half years' imprisonment (*Index* 4/1999). The sentence, imposed for establishing a syndicate of independent journalists, effectively sanctions the government-backed journalist union as the only medium for representation. (*Cairo Times*)

On 14 August a criminal court sentenced the editor-in-chief of *Al-Shaab* newspaper, **Magdy Hussein**, **Salah Bedewi**, a board member of the Hussein and the cartoonist **Essam Hanafi** each to two-year terms of imprisonment and LE20,000 fines (*Index* 3/1998, 4/1998, 5/1998, 6/1998, 4/1999). Another *Al-Shaab* journalist, **Adel Hussein**, who is secretary general of Al-Amal political party, was fined LE20,000 in the same case of slander brought by the minister of agriculture and deputy prime minister Yussef Wali against *Al-Shaab*. (Egyptian Organisation for Human Rights)

ETHIOPIA

Editor of *Mebruk* newspaper **Tesehalene Mengesh**, jailed since 5 March for publishing articles critical of the government, was released on bail on 7 June. (IFJ)

Journalists **Garuma Bekele, Solomon Nemerra** and **Tesfaye Deressa**, of *Urji* newspaper, were charged on 4 July with violating press law. They were denied bail because they had also been charged with engaging in 'terrorist activities'. The total number of journalists now in prison stands at 11. (IFJ)

FIJI

On 3 June journalists were informed that they would not be allowed to approach members of Bose Levu Vakaturaga (Great Council of Chiefs) during breaks. The *Fiji*

Times commented: 'At least in the past reporters were permitted to talk to the chiefs during breaks in an effort to glean at least some idea of what is going on. Now even that is banned.' (Pacific Islands News Association)

On 25 July **Ken Clark**, the new chief executive of state-owned Fiji Television, was granted an extension to his temporary work permit, which will enable him to appeal against the newly elected Labour-led government's decision to ask him to leave the island. He was told the decision was made because the company had not attempted to train a local to replace the former chief executive. Prime Minister Mahendra Chaudry has said his government is looking at terminating the contracts of all expatriates, including those working in the media, and replacing them with locals. (Pacific Islands News Association)

The *Fiji Times* has claimed that, at an 11 June caucus meeting of Prime Minister Mahendra Chaudhry's Labour Party, a police officer guarding Chaudhry pushed a Fiji TV camera operator away, pulled another reporter and attempted to push a third. Assistant information minister Lekh Ram Vayeshnoi promised to look into the behaviour of the security personnel. Chaudhry is also Fiji's information minister. (Pacific Islands News Association)

FRANCE

On 10 June the National Assembly finally acknowledged

fighting the Algerian war between 1954 and 1962, when in a unanimous vote it abandoned the official claim that the eight-year struggle between Algerian nationalists and French troops had been no more than 'an operation for keeping order'. (*Daily Telegraph*)

In July President Jacques Chirac refused a revision of the constitution necessary for the State to ratify the European Charter of Regional and Minority Languages. The decision angered many Bretons and has fuelled a national revival in the region. Native speakers of the Breton language have since threatened to secede and apply for British citizenship in protest. (*Daily Telegraph*)

On 28 July France became the first country to be convicted of torture by the European Court of Human Rights in Strasbourg. The torture occurred from 25 to 29 November 1991 when **Ahmed Selmouni**, a Moroccan-Dutch dual national, was detained by police in Bobigny. Selmouni alleged that he was kicked and beaten with fists and a baseball bat, his toes were crushed and he was chained to stairs in an attempt to force a confession to smuggling heroin. He is currently serving a 15-year sentence imposed in 1992. (*Irish Times*, AI)

FRENCH POLYNESIA

On 10 June **Vito Maamaatua**, news director of the pro-independence radio station Te Reo o Tefana, accused the government of retaining a partial gag on the media. He also said that journalists from the state-run RFO are given angles for their news stories and prevented from covering important issues. 'You will have to learn to read between the lines because [the media] will never write the truth, it is very rare.' In April, French Polynesian President Gaston Flosse lifted a seven-year ban on the radio station that had prevented it from attending government news conferences. (Pacific Media Watch)

GAMBIA

The newly launched *Independent* newspaper was suspended in late July following publication in its debut issue of 5 July of an opposition United Democratic Party (UDP) statement accusing President Yahya Jammeh of being 'the most corrupt head of state in Africa'. The ministry of justice claimed the suspension was due to 'irregularities on its enrolment in the trade Department'. Three *Independent* journalists, **Baba Galleh Jallow, Yorro Jallow** and **Lamin Daffeh,** were detained at the National Intelligence Agency headquarters on 2 August in connection with the closure. (RSF)

GEORGIA

The widespread mistrust of Jehovah's Witnesses reached a climax in mid-June in the southern district of Akhaltsikhe, when 100 Orthodox Christians picketed police headquarters demanding the destruction of six tonnes of the sect's religious tracts and video cassettes confiscated by customs in late April (*Index* 4/1999). Despite calls from the Georgian Orthodox Patriarchate to outlaw

Jehovah's Witnesses and institute Georgian Orthodox Christianity as the state religion, reports in late July indicated that the government would resist such measures. (RFE/RL, Caucasian Institute for Peace, Democracy and Development, *Resonance*)

It was reported on 23 July that Tbilisi police plan to shave the heads of pickpockets who are caught in the act. The police believe that they have the legal right to do so, but the legal ombudsman has suggested that such punishments would violate human rights. (*Caucasus Press*)

The first issue of *Glavezh* ('Morning Star'), a monthly newspaper for the Yezidi Kurdish community, was published on 12 August. Publisher and editor **Karam Ankos** (a Yezid theologian) stressed the newspaper's apolitical character. Between 30,000 and 60,000 of Georgia's Kurdish population are adherents of the Yezidi religion. (Caucasus Press, Caucasian Institute for Peace, Democracy and Development)

HONDURAS

Two TELENISA journalists, **Renato Alvarez** and **Cesar Omar Silva Rosales**, have faced intimidation and harassment for their forthright coverage of the escalating unrest within the military and police establishments since the September 1998 appointment of the civilian minister of defence, Edguardo Dumas Rodriguez. The news director for Channel 63, Alvarez was threatened by two men at his home in Tegucigalpa on 30 July. The

following day, Rosales, a TELENISA reporter, noticed that he was being followed home from work by a group of men in a car with no number plates. It is believed that the men were attempting to discover Rosales' home address. (AI)

INDIA

On 5 July it was reported that Videsh Sanchar Nigam Ltd (VSNL), the country's sole gateway to the Internet, had been blocking the website of Pakistan's leading English-language daily, *Dawn*, for over a week. VSNL acknowledged that the site was unavailable but denied that it had been deliberately blocked because of the Kargil dispute with Pakistan. In June, information and broadcasting minister Pramod Mahajan banned cable operators from showing Pakistan TV (*Index* 4/1999). (Pakistan Press Foundation, *Times of India*)

On 22 July copies of **Arundhati Roy**'s book *The Greatest Common Good* were burned by Youth Congress members in the state of Gujarat because of its trenchant critique of the Sardar Sarovar dam project. The party threatened all bookstores in the state with demonstrations if they failed to withdraw the publication from their shelves. One week later, the Supreme Court began deliberations on whether to initiate contempt of court proceedings against Roy for publishing the book, on the grounds that it is 'an attempt to undermine the dignity of the court and influence the course of justice'. (*Times of India*, CPJ)

Recent Publication: *India Against Itself: Assam And The Politics Of Nationality* by Sanjib Baruah (University of Pennsylvania Press, 1999, pp 257).

INDONESIA

On 8 June three journalists were banned from 'freely pursuing press activities' in the office of the Attorney General Andi Ghalib, following claims that they had 'acted inappropriately by making accusatory statements directed at the Attorney General and questioning in an interrogatory manner at a press conference'. **Bambang Wahyu** from the leading daily *Kompas*, **Roy Pakpahan** of the *Suara Bangsa* daily and **Driantama** from RCTI private television, learnt of the decision via an oral statement and were told the ban would be in place for an undefined period. (Association of Independent Journalists, Agence France-Presse)

On 14 June the UN Assistance Mission in East Timor (UNAMET) began broadcasting news and feature reports in five languages in the lead-up to the 31 August referendum on possible independence from Indonesian rule. The hour-long broadcasts, repeated three times a day under an agreement with Radio Republic Indonesia (RRI), stressed the secrecy of the impending ballot (Australian Associated Press, Pacific Islands News Association)

A former pro-Indonesian militia commander has claimed that information minister Yunus Yosfiah had a direct role in the killing of five western newsmen during the 1975 invasion of East Timor, the *Sydney Morning Herald* reported on 21 June. According to an article by freelance writer **Jill Jolliffe**, who has covered East Timor for 25 years: 'the commander said he had watched the unarmed journalists standing outside a house in the town of Balibo as the then Captain Yunus and soldiers under his command opened fire on them. He said Mr Yunus had ignored their pleas for mercy as they fell in a hail of bullets.' The unidentified commander is seeking political asylum in Australia. Now one of the most influential members of the Habibie government, Yunus has consistently denied any knowledge of the killing on 16 October, 1975, of **Greg Shackleton**, **Gary Cunningham** and **Tony Stewart** of Channel 7, and **Brian Peters** and **Malcolm Rennie** of Channel 9 although he was commander in Balibo at the time of the attack. (*Sydney Morning Herald*, Pacific Islands News Association)

A military inquiry into charges of bribery against Sri Roso Sudarmo failed to explore the more serious case of the 13 August 1996 murder of *Bernas* journalist **Fuad Muhammad**, also known as **Udin**, whose investigations had incriminated the former regent of Bantul (*Index* 5/1996). It was strongly suspected then that Muhammad was murdered because of his criticisms of Sri Roso. But in the trial which began on 22 June, Sri Roso stands accused only of attempting to bribe the Dharmais Foundation, chaired by former President Suharto, to the tune of one billion rupiah (approximately US$149,107). The legal head of the IV/Diponegoro Military Command, Colonel Sukirno, said that there was no connection between this case and Udin's murder and the district military commander, Major General Bibit Waluyo, has tried to reduce the charge to one of 'violation of the oath of service'. (*Kompas*, Association of Independent Journalists)

Early in the morning of 10 August, unidentified assailants threw two Molotov cocktails at the home in Banda Aceh of **Sjamsul Kahar**, chief editor of the Aceh-based, Indonesian-language daily newspaper *Serambi Indonesia* and chairman of the Aceh chapter of the Association of Indonesian Journalists, setting his car ablaze. No-one was injured, but Kahar left Aceh the next day. Kahar has received death threats almost weekly since May when violence in Aceh between Indonesian soldiers and separatist rebels escalated sharply. (CPJ)

Supriadi, a journalist with North Sumatra's *Medan Pos* newspaper, was found hacked to death on 5 August in Buki Hagu village in North Aceh district. His wife said that he had been abducted from their house late on 3 August by two unidentified men. *Medan Pos*' chief editor said Supriadi had been working on stories about corruption in an agricultural project for small farmers. (RSF)

IRAN

Hossein Kachani, director of the reformist weekly *Hoviyat-e-*

Khich, was arrested on 16 June, followed by his colleague, **Hechmatollah Tabarzadi**, one day later. Both were held at Evin prison and Tarbazadi is reported to have been tortured. The newspaper is accused of publishing 'false and insulting information' in two articles relating to the riots in Iraqi Kurdistan following the capture of Abdullah Ocalan, and the role of the judiciary in the murder of Iranian dissidents in late 1998. Tarbazadi's associates **Mohammad Massod Salamati**, **Seyed Djavad Emami** and **Parviz Safari** were also arrested on or around 13 July. (AI, RSF)

On 7 July the conservative-dominated Majlis (Legislature) gave preliminary approval to a new press law that compels journalists to reveal their sources and bars opposition journalists and editors from 'any form of press activities'. It also criminalises the journalistic profession by making reporters personally liable for what they write and placing 'national security-related' press offences under the jurisdiction of Iran's hard-line revolutionary court, rather than the press courts. (CPJ, Agence France Presse)

The same day, a court ordered *Salam* to cease publication, following a complaint by the intelligence ministry that the paper had printed on 6 July details of an alleged official plot to restrict journalistic expression in Iran. *Salam* journalist **Morad Veissi** was arrested and the director **Mohamad Mousavi-Khoeiniha** was charged. On 25 July *Salam* was ordered to suspend publication for five years. Khoeiniha was given a three-year suspension from journalism for publishing an allegedly classified document; slandering provincial officials; and linking members of parliament to a 'rogue secret agent' accused of masterminding the murder of several dissidents last year (*Index* 1/1999, 2/1999, 3/1999, 4/1999). (CPJ)

Kazem Shokri, editor of the moderate daily *Sobh Emrooz*, was arrested on 20 July and charged with having authorised the publication of an article offensive to the Quran. On the same day **Saeed Hajarian**, managing director of the newspaper, was summoned to court over an article entitled 'Two parallel lines do not cross unless God wills it'. He was later released on bail. (WiPC, RSF, PEN)

IRAQ

The ruling Ba'ath party newspaper reported on 7 July that citizens are now allowed to own and install fax machines in their own homes. (*Daily Telegraph*)

IRELAND

On 23 July the minister for finance Charlie McCreevy stated at a press conference that details of the National Development Plan, the most wide-ranging in the history of the state, would be kept secret until it is finalised in late September or early October. He said he would not publish to allow a public debate, as the process of drawing up the plan had to 'come to an end some time ago'. (*Irish Times*)

On 12 August the entertainment listings magazine *In Dublin* was banned by the little-known Censorship of Publications Board for six months for 'containing lewd and obscene material'. It is understood that the complainant was offended not only by the magazine's 'controversial' advertisements for 'massage parlours' and 'health studios', but also some of the magazine covers and an advertisement for a condom manufacturer. (*Irish Times, Irish Independent*)

ITALY

An elderly prelate, **Monsignor Luigi Marinelli**, 73, faces trial in a religious court over his book *Gone With The Wind in the Vatican*, it was reported in late July. The book, which has sold more than 100,000 copies since publication in February, is a sex and corruption *roman à clef* of life in the corridors of the Holy See. The Vatican denied it was trying to gag free thought, saying its action is intended to 'protect those smeared by calumny'. If found guilty Marinelli will be stripped of his 'priestly prerogatives', his book will be removed from sale and all translations stopped. (*Daily Telegraph*)

On 13 July the Vatican ordered an American priest and nun to end a ministry for gay men and lesbians, arguing they had strayed from the church teaching that homosexuality is 'intrinsically disordered' and 'evil'. The decision came after a decade of investigation into the pair's work with gay and lesbian Catholics since the 1970s. (*New York Times*)

SA'ID ESIAMI
Proposal to amend the Press Law

' As Your Excellency is aware, the extensive activities undertaken by
elements such as Golshiri, Chehel-Tan, Dolatabadi and Mokhtari ...
aimed at keeping the [Writers'] Association in the news, raising its profile in the
world and gaining international support, will cause security problems for the
Islamic Republic of Iran and, especially, this ministry.

The existence of parallel legal currents and the establishment of plants with
the aim of fomenting schisms and sowing discord among them can diminish the
threat to security.

Amending the current Press Law would not be enough in itself to thwart
the existing plots because it only holds licence-holders and managing directors
responsible; whereas, in the cultural arena, we are faced with a wide-ranging
group of writers, translators, publishers, reporters, poets and ... whose attacks
can only be prevented by confronting them individually, using the law, in order
to ban them from writing or publishing.

To this end, it is hereby recommended that the honourable deputy minister's
department should set out to draw up a draft members' bill or government bill
similar to ... the country's culture, in order to ensure that we have the required
lever to lend legality to the security measures. The bill must include such issues
as the professional nature of the work and eligibility for it (on the condition of
having the required qualifications, as is the case with doctors or lawyers), such
that the relevant person can be given an identification number under the
cultural system, deeming them to be a translator or a writer; [and] the
establishment of a special court (disciplinary in nature) which would deal with
offences committed by these people and carry out the required sentencing. In
this way, associations that are acceptable to us can be strengthened and hostile
elements driven away.

'The cultural system can embrace the field of books, the press, theatre,
cinema, music and so on ...'

*Sa'id Eslami was one of the intelligence ministry officials arrested for the killing of
writers and opposition figures in 1998 (*Index 1/1999, 2/1999, 3/1999). *The above
is extracted from a report called* The Cultural Climate and its Control. *It formed the
lead story in the Tehran daily* Salam *on 6 July and led to its banning a day later. Sa'id
Eslami reportedly attempted suicide in prison on 16 June 1999 and died three days later.
Translated by Nilou Mobasser*

IVORY COAST

Journalists **Raphael Lakpe** and **Jean Khalil Sylla** were jailed on 28 April and 9 June respectively following the publication in the *Le Populaire* newspaper of an article on the killing and wounding of students during a confrontation with police. (RSF)

JORDAN

On 30 June **Shaker al-Jawhari**, editor-in-chief of the daily *Al-'Arab al-Yawm* and Chef de Bureau of the *Al-Khaleej* daily, was released after one day's questioning by the General Intelligence Department in Amman. He said that he was asked about an interview with the Palestinian leader 'Abu Daoud' which was considered 'injurious' to the State; a report on the quality of hospital services; and his position towards the policies of the present government. (RSF)

On 13 July '**Abdul Hadi Majali**, a writer for *Al-'Arab al-Yawm* daily, was hospitalised following an attack by unknown assailants while on his way home from work. The paper, whose criticisms of the government had soared in recent weeks, said that the attack coincided with an anti-*Al-'Arab al-Yawm* campaign launched by other local dailies and the Jordan News Agency. (*Jordan Times*)

On 10 August journalist **Sinan Shadiqh**, senior adviser to the evening daily *Al-Massa'iyah* and senior corresponding editor for the Emirates daily *Al-Ittihad*, was released after over two weeks' detention at Jweidah prison

where he was questioned about several of his articles. The State Security Court charged him with 'harming ties with a neighbouring country', namely Syria. Despite his release Shaqdih was unaware as to whether the charges had been dropped. (AMIN)

KAZAKSTAN

Yevgeniy Kosenko, a journalist working for the newly opened Almaty newspaper *Vremya*, was badly beaten by unknown assailants in front of his house on 23 June. Kosenko had been documenting corruption among private fuel stations in Almaty. (RFE/RL)

The Almaty newspaper *Nachnem s Ponedelenika* was forced to close from 24 to 30 June because its bank accounts had been frozen by the Almaty City Justice. The accounts were frozen earlier in 1999 following a successful 50 million tenge (US$308,000) claim for 'moral damages' against the paper by local businessman Marat Oqshibayev. Information Minister Altynbek Sarsembaev reportedly intervened to lift the freeze on the newspaper's funds. However, newspaper staff were back in court on 4 August accused of having published false statements critical of the Almaty City Court. (RFE/RL)

Bigeldin Gabdullin, editor-in-chief of the Almaty-based opposition newspaper *XXI Vek* ('21st Century'), was summoned to a meeting at the Hotel Otrar on 19 July at which a man who identified himself as a member of the Kazak State Security Service (KNB) screened a

videotape purporting to show Gabdullin taking a bribe. The KNB agent told Gabdullin that the videotape would be aired on national television unless *XXI Vek* stopped criticising the government. Gabdullin denied ever accepting a bribe and refused the deal. On 21 July, the KTK commercial TV channel aired a segment showing Gabdullin receiving a wad of cash from an unseen figure beyond camera range; Gabdullin contended that the clip shows a legitimate exchange of money between Gabdullin and a shareholder in the paper. He has demanded that KTK back up the allegations in the accompanying commentary that Gabdullin had received money from a State Security Service agent. (CPJ)

Seydakhmet Quttyqadam, who heads the Orleu (Progress) Party, told journalists in Almaty on 28 July that he has been formally charged with insulting President Nursultan Nazarbaev. The charge relates to Quttyqadam's comments at a rally in February that Nazarbaev should resign, having failed to fulfil his obligations as president. (RFE/RL)

KENYA

On 10 August Kwanza MP **George Kapten** was charged with slander and 'undermining' presidential authority following a magazine interview in which he accused President Daniel arap Moi of masterminding the Goldenberg gold fraud in the mid-1990s. (*Daily Nation*, Media Institute)

People Daily journalist **Benson**

Wambugu and photographer **Joseph Waweru** narrowly escaped death on 3 August when they were attacked by over 50 coffee farm workers. Both men, and their driver **Julius Wanjohi**, suffered multiple injuries when they were caught in between two rival factions trying to control a coffee estate in Central province. (Ndima)

Journalist **Tony Gachoka** (*Index* 3/1999) was charged with contempt of court when he returned from exile. The charge arose from articles he published in the 6 February edition of the *Post on Sunday* which implicated the judiciary in the Goldenberg gold scandal. (Media Institute)

KUWAIT

Journalists **Fawwaz Muhammad al-Awadhi Bseiso** and **Ibtisam Berto Sulaiman al-Daakhil** of the *An-Nidaa* newspaper remain inexplicably detained despite the release of three of their colleagues on 25 February. The five were originally sentenced to death for alleged collaboration with occupying Iraqi forces during the Second Gulf War, but the sentences were later commuted to life imprisonment. (WAN)

KYRGYZSTAN

An appeal hearing in the libel conviction of the opposition weekly *Res Publica*, scheduled for 8 July, was postponed indefinitely by the Supreme Court when the claimant, National Television and Radio Corporation president Amanbek Karypkulov, failed to appear. Earlier this year, Karypkulov was awarded 200,000 soms (US$5,000) compensation by a district court for the 'insult to his honour and dignity' caused by a open letter of complaint from 20 employees that was published in *Res Publica*'s 12 January edition (*Index* 3/1999, 4/1999). (RFE/RL)

A 16 July Supreme Court decision found that pro-government journalist **Kalen Sydykova** had not libelled parliamentary deputy Ishenbai Kadyrbekov when she wrote in a 1998 article that there were criminals holding parliamentary seats and criticised Kadyrbekov's 'shady enterprises'. The Supreme Court decision reinstated a district court verdict that had later been overturned by Bishkek City Court. (RFE/RL)

LEBANON

On 30 July it was reported that two journalists were facing legal proceedings for interviewing Robert Hatem (pseudonym Cobra), author of the banned book *From Israel to Damascus*. **Melhem Karam** and **Said Nassereddine**, editor and editor-in-chief respectively of the daily *Al-Baryak*, face two-month sentences for violating a press law. Similar proceedings are also in action against **Paul Elie Salem** and **Jamil Kamel Mroue**, owner and editor-in-chief repectively of the monthly the *Lebanon Report*, for publishing excerpts from the book. (RSF)

Antoun Khoury Harb and **Bassem Youssef** were reportedly arrested without warrant on 1 August while distributing flyers protesting against the army. It is believed that they are being held by security forces in Tripoli and that Harb at least has been denied access to a lawyer. (OMCT)

MALAWI

Four senior radio employees at the state-owned Malawi Broadcasting Corporation (MBC) were fired on 23 June, apparently for criticising the ruling USF party. According to a report in the *Daily Times*, **Geoffrey Msampha**, **Patrick Mphaka**, **Laston Rusk Nkwapatira** and **Tom Chiuse** were dismissed 'after their workmates reported to management that they are opposition supporters'. The article went on to say that the four were aware of their imminent dismissal even before the 15 June election. Sources quoted by the *Times* said that the firing of the four had sent shock waves through the corporation. 'Just a mere negative joke against the ruling UDF party can cost someone a job here,' one source was quoted as saying. (Media Institute of Southern Africa)

On 21 June police in Blantyre arrested **Horace Somanje**, editor of the weekly *Malawi News*, and reporter **Mabvuto Banda** for allegedly inciting the military to take over the country. The detentions stemmed from an article in the 19 June edition which quoted angry opposition supporters calling for 'the army to take over' because President Bakili

Muluzi and his United Democratic Front had rigged the 15 June elections. (Media Institute of Southern Africa)

MEXICO

Concerns for the safety of **Jesus Barraza**, editor of the weekly magazine *Pulso* in San Luis Rió Colorado, escalated on 5 June (*Index* 4/1999). Angered by his coverage of drug trafficking in the region, Federal Judicial Police (PFJ) attacked Barraza's police bodyguard who subsequently withdrew and refused to provide any further protection. The previous week Barraza had published an article calling for an investigation into alleged links between the PJF and local drug traffickers. (CPJ)

MOROCCO

The government banned the 28 July edition of the satirical French weekly *Le Canard Enchaîné* following its front-page story on the death of King Hassan. (RSF)

MOZAMBIQUE

On 13 July **Felisberto Arnaca**, a journalist working for the daily *Noticias*, was assaulted in Maputo City Hall by a parliamentary official, Valgy Tricamugy, while covering a special meeting of the Parliamentary Forum of the Portuguese Speaking Countries. Sources said Tricamugy accused Arnaca of having entered his office and stolen a document belonging to a member of the Angolan delegation which contained information about the military situation in Angola. Arnaca says that the document

was given to him by the Angolans. (Media Institute of Southern Africa)

NAMIBIA

The Lozi-language service of the Namibian Broadcasting Corporation (NBC), based in Katima Mulilo in Caprivi province, ceased broadcasting on 2 August following the occupation of the building by alleged secessionist rebels. The Namibian Defence Force later blasted the building with mortars in an attempt to dislodge the attackers. Reports suggested that the attackers tried to go on air but did not succeed. There were no reports of casualties among NBC staff. (Media Institute of Southern Africa)

NIGERIA

Phillips Umbago, a computer operator with the News Agency of Nigeria, was reported missing on 28 May. (Nigerian Media Monitor)

Freelance journalist **Edward Olaleken Ayo-Ojo** was found dead beside his car on a Lagos road in the early hours of 1 June. An autopsy on the former news editor failed to find the cause of death, though locals suggested he had been strangled. Ayo-Ojo had worked with several papers including the *Daily Times*. (RSF)

Journalist **Sam Ninta Jan**, correspondent with a Ja-based magazine, was reportedly macheted to death during disturbances following the official installation of Alhaji Isa Mohammadu Mohammed as

the new Emir of Jemaa. (Nigerian Media Monitor)

On 29 June **Adewale Adeoye**, assistant news editor with the *Punch* newspaper, petitioned the Lagos State Governor, Mr. Bola Tinubu, over his torture, arrest and detention by the police run anti-crime outfit, Rapid Response Squad. (Independent Journalism Centre)

On 21 July **Toyin Coker**, a journalist for African Independent Television, was arrested by police in Ogun state, scene of clashes between Yoruba and Hausa peoples over housing. Coker was reportedly interrogated, tortured and released the following day. (Independent Journalism Centre)

On 30 July the management of Independent Communications Network Limited (ICNL), publishers of *The News* magazine, stated that they had been receiving unusual telephone calls threatening the magazine's officials. In a statement, ICNL said that at about 10:00 p.m. (local time) on 29 July: 'a call came to our office, through a line which has never been published and which is known only to a select few of our staff. The caller said: "You should stop what you are doing, if not, we are going to kill you. In fact, we are coming to your house tonight."' The statement noted that the calls became incessant after the company published an investigative story on allegations of forgery and perjury against Alhaji Salisu Buhari, the speaker of the House of Representatives, in the 19 July edition of *The News*.

Buhari subsequently resigned from his position. (Independent Journalism Centre)

PAKISTAN

Shortly after his release from prison and the dropping of sedition charges against him on 2 June, **Najam Sethi** (*Index* 4/1999), editor-in-chief of the *Friday Times*, accused the government income tax department of intimidating him and his wife **Jugno Moshin**. According to Sethi, over two dozen notices have been filed against him, his wife, the *Friday Times* and Vanguard Books, his publishing company. On 23 June Sethi was prevented from boarding a flight to London, where he was due to accept an Amnesty International award. On 15 July he was summoned to appear in court on 28 July by the Chief Election Commissioner (CEC), in response to a petition filed by Syed Zafar Ali, a member of the ruling party, who wants to bar Sethi from ever voting or running for political office. The petition asked the CEC to assess Sethi's 'religious credentials', requesting that his name be struck from the voters list if he did 'not meet the [constitutional] requirements of a Muslim'. (CPJ, Pakistan Press Foundation)

Editor of the weekly magazine *Pakistan News* **Naveed Shah Arain**, and staff writer **Nisar Mehmood**, were arrested in Karachi on 8 July for publishing an article that could 'disturb sectarian harmony'. Police ransacked the magazine's offices and seized copies of the edition from newsagents throughout

Sindh province. On 9 July both journalists were released on 'medical grounds'. The editor of the Sindhi edition of the magazine claimed the actions were taken because *Pakistan News* had regularly published articles on police corruption. (Pakistan Press Foundation)

PALESTINE

On 23 April it was reported that a postage stamp commemorating the Wye Accords had cropped Benjamin Netanyahu out of a picture of Yasser Arafat and President Bill Clinton. Palestine National Authority (PNA) postal services head Omar Magdadi explained that 'It is a stamp commemorating those who have invested a lot of effort in peace.' (*London Jewish Chronicle*)

On 3 and 20 July, freelance journalist **Maher al-Alami** was summoned to the police station in Ramallah, questioned for several hours and allegedly threatened regarding a number of articles for the Gaza-based weekly *Al-Istiqlal*. The articles had focused on apparent embezzlement within the PNA. (RSF)

On 5 August, following the publication of his article entitled 'The Battle Goes On' in *People's Rights Magazine*, **Dr Eyad Sarraj**, director of the Gaza Community Mental Health Programme, was questioned by civilian police. The article criticised recent PNA attacks on human rights NGOs. He was released on bail, with travel restrictions, while investigations against him continue. Dr al-Sarraj was previously arrested on

7 December 1995, 18 May 1996, and 9 June 1996, always in connection with statements critical of the self-rule government and its security forces. (AMIN)

PARAGUAY

On 23 June Judge Norma Jara de Benitez passed a 'disciplinary arrest' sentence against journalists **Nino Silguero** and **Norma Acuna** at the Court of Appeal. Apparently, the journalists were accused by the judge of insulting her on air, but both state they were simply reporting on comments made against her during a demonstration by workers in support of two colleagues imprisoned for 'disturbing public peace'. (RSF)

PERU

Jaime Antonio Angulo Quesquen, journalist and owner of Radio Stereo Laser Plus in Pacasmayo province, was subjected to threats and intimidation throughout May and June by state official Carlos Vera Cepeda and businessman Eduardo Burgos Delgado. The journalist's reports on irregularities in Vera's state post had led to his dismissal. On 14 May Angulo was physically threatened when his home was broken into by Vera and Burgos while, on 7 June, the radio premises were vandalised by unknown individuals. (Instituto de Prensa y Sociedad)

Journalist **Felix Haro Rodriguez**, of Radio 1160's affiliate in Aucayacu, was found dead days after disappearing on 2 June. He appeared to have been killed with machetes and his body had been dismembered. Although his radio programme featured traditional music and was aimed at local villagers, he also informed listeners of corruption, terrorist violence and drug trafficking in the region. The nature of his murder is consistent with the rebel *Sendero Luminoso* ('Shining Path') movement. (Instituto de Prensa y Sociedad, IPI)

On 7 June the newspaper *La República* brought a case against the publishers of the 'false' newspaper *Repudica* to the public prosecutor. Although only one edition of *Repudica* was published on 31 May (*Index* 4/1998, 1/1999, 4/1999), *La República* charged that *Repudica* copied its style, format and page design in an attempt to disparage independent journalists and opponents of the government. While the Institute for the Defence of Consumers and Intellectual Property (INDECOPI) prohibited the distribution and marketing of the fake paper on 9 June, charges against *Repudica*'s executive director, **Arturo Caceres**, were shelved less than three weeks later. In late July, editions of a new defamatory publication called *Repudio,* of which Caceres is also director, appeared on the shelves and continued the smear campaign against the editor of *La República*, **Gustavo Mohme Llona**. (Instituto de Prensa y Sociedad, IFJ)

Rosa Vallejos was sentenced on 8 June to a conditional one-year prison term and a fine of 5,000 soles (US$1,500) in civil damages for 'crimes against honour'. Vallejos was a journalist with the magazine *Caretas*, when her July 1998 article reported on the circumstances of a former state official, Luis Augusto Alarcon Schroder, being charged with murder. She was convicted for not mentioning that Alarcon had been acquitted of the charge in 1992. (Instituto de Prensa y Sociedad)

On 9 June **Hector Ricardo Faisal Fracalossi** appeared in court in Lima to respond to charges of posting articles on the internet which defamed a group of independent journalists. Faisal is the legal representative of the Association for the Defence of the Truth. On 26 July, he was absolved of all charges. (IFJ, Instituto de Prensa y Sociedad)

On 9 June the government closed Radio HGV studios in the province of Santa Cruz, claiming it was operating without a licence. The station's press manager believes the action was in response to the watchdog role HGV plays in the community. (Instituto de Prensa y Sociedad)

On 27 June journalist **Marco Antonio Cossio Vega**, director of the *La Voz del Pueblo* programme on Radio Mix, was attacked by six unknown individuals. According to the radio station, the incident may be linked to Cossio's reporting of administrative irregularities committed by the province's mayor. (Instituto de Prensa y Sociedad)

At the end of June, Radio Maranon journalists in Jaen began receiving telephone threats and were subjected to harassment. The station's producer, **Jose Luis Linares,** was also threatened on 10 July by two individuals, one of whom he recognised as having attempted to kill him at his home on 18 March. On 16 July, *La República* newspaper and *Caretas* magazine both reported that the Radio Maranon journalists had been followed by army personnel. (Instituto de Prensa y Sociedad)

Journalists **Abel Robles Veliz** and **Nelly Castro Pachari** of Radio Studio 99, and **Jorge Luis Romero Mendoza** of Radio Sideral, were physically assaulted at a meeting between the re-elected mayor, Arturo Durand Panez and his supporters. The journalists were covering the meeting held on 2 July to discuss a protest demonstration being planned against the provincial judge, the public prosecutor attorney general and the press. (Instituto de Prensa y Sociedad)

On 14 July the state announced it would no longer accept the jurisdiction of the Inter-American Court of Human Rights. This move came as several pending issues awaited decisions both in the Court and at the Inter-American Commission of Human Rights. The Commission has criticised the government for revoking the citizenship of the former president of the television station Frecuencia Latina, **Baruch Ivcher,** in 1997 and for refusing to allow journalists, currently on trial, access to an independent hearing (*Index* 4/1997, 6/1997, 1/1999,

2/1998, 3/1998, 4/1998, 5/1998, 6/1998, 2/1999, 4/1999). (*New York Times, Washington Post,* RSF)

A new legal case was opened at the end of July against **Baruch Ivcher** accusing him of misusing capital resources, fraud and 'causing harm' to his old television station, Frecuencia Latina. It the sixth legal case against him. (Instituto de Prensa y Sociedad)

On 14 June the cultural editor of the Belgian newspaper *De Morgen*, **Eric Bracke**, was kidnapped with **Lieven de Marche**, a friend working for the Belgian Foreign Aid Programme, while travelling on a boating trip to the island of Santa Cruz. The MILF, the main Muslim separatist movement in the area, denied any responsibility. Bracke was on holiday at the time. (IFJ)

On 29 July the president of the Movement for Press Freedom, **Ed Aurelio Reyes**, warned of 'a creeping resurgence of martial rule' following the withdrawal of advertising from the *Philippine Daily Inquirer* and the sale of the *Manila Times*, both of which were critical of President Joseph Estrada. The *Manila Times* is believed to have been purchased by business associates of Estrada (*Index* 4/1999), but he dismissed stories that copies of its last issue, before the change of ownership, had been confiscated as a 'gimmick to boost sales'. On 26 July the National Press Club board of directors stated that the decision by a number of movie producers to pull

advertising revenue from the *Inquirer* was not intended to curtail press freedom. President Estrada is a former movie actor and a close ally of the movie industry. (PMPF)

On 5 June, Pope John Paul met **Father Henryk Jankowski**, former chaplain to ex-Polish President Lech Walesa in Gdansk. Jankowski had served a one-year ban on preaching in 1997 as a result of his anti-Semitic remarks. He said that Jews had no place in Polish government and last year, he warned voters in local elections to check if candidates were Russians or Jews before casting their votes. (*Yahoo News*)

The co-author of a newspaper report on radiation hazards in the Northern Fleet, **Aleksandr Nikitin**, was charged on 2 July with high treason and divulging State secrets for the eighth successive time in St Petersburg. The Security Police indicted Nikitin with a 'damage assessment' to the security of the Federation of a cost of US$1 million, despite the Supreme Court's view that the figure was 'incomprehensible'. The case is expected to reach court in October this year. (Bellona Foundation)

On 20 July the Russian military 'finally admitted its mistake of imprisoning an innocent man for over one and a half years' after they released naval captain **Grigory Pasko**, reporter for *Boyevaya Vakhta* – the newspaper of the Russian military fleet –

who was jailed in November 1997 for espionage and revealing State secrets. In 1993 Pasko had filmed a navy tanker dumping radioactive waste in the Sea of Japan, footage which was then broadcast by Japanese TV station NHK and by a station in Primorsky Krai, eastern Russia. Pasko was released by the Russian Pacific Fleet military court after it found the prosecution lacked evidence to support the charges against him, although he was found guilty of 'abuse of office, and sentenced to the maximum imprisonment of three years. (WAN, CPJ, AI)

On 3 August the home of the manager of television station Kanal 4 in the Ekaterinburg region of the Urals was attacked by unknown individuals with hand grenades which completely destroyed the apartment. **Igor Michine** was not at home at the time of the attack. The Kanal 4 station is owned by the Most financial group, which support Moscow mayor Youri Loujkov, one of the candidates in the race to replace President Boris Yeltsin. On 2 August 14 editors-in-chief sent a letter to the presidential administration denouncing the pressure under which the media are subject from 'high-ranking officials' in the pre-election campaign period. (RSF, RFE/RL)

Editor-in-chief of the influential *Kommersant Daily*, **Raf Shakirov**, was dismissed on 4 August claiming financier Boris Berezovski, who recently acquired a 15% stake in the Kommersant publishing house, was behind his removal. According to Shakirov,

Berezovski is likely to run for the state Duma. The *Nezavisimaya Gazeta*, a newspaper funded by Berezovski's LogoVaz group, had predicted Shakirov would be dismissed and replaced with someone loyal to Berezovski. The *Gazeta* also reported the current editor of government newspaper *Rossiiskaya Gazeta* would be replaced by Andrei Shtorkh, currently a consultant to Boris Yeltsin. (RFE/RL)

RWANDA

Valerie Bemeriki, a female journalist accused of leading a campaign of hate that fuelled the 1994 genocide, was arrested on 21 June. Her name appears in a list of the 1,000 most wanted leaders of the genocide against minority Tutsis and Hutu sympathisers. (Reuters)

SERBIA-MONTENEGRO

On 7 June Kosovar Albanian journalist **Cerkin Ibishi** was reported to have turned up in Albania following his arrest near Mitrovica in the first week of May. A journalist who spoke with Ibishi said he had spent time in two prisons and showed signs of having been abused and tortured while in detention. (HRW)

On 9 June the daily and weekly Serbian editions of *Nezavisne Novine*, a newspaper close to the government of Prime Minister Milorad Dodik, were seized at the Serb-Yugoslav border by police. The following day copies of the daily edition were again seized. **Gradisa Katic,** editor-in-chief of *Nezavisne Novine*, claimed 'the chief reason for the

seizure is that our newspaper quotes a number of politicians who stated that the Belgrade regime was going to surrender'. (RSF)

On 10 June **Antun Masle**, a correspondent for the independent Croatian weekly *Globus*, escaped from the custody of Yugoslav federal troops in Montenegro and fled to Croatia. The 40-year-old war correspondent evaded his guards in a Podgorica hospital, where he had been transferred from prison after complaining of stomach pains. Masle was arrested by Yugoslav officers on 20 April and then imprisoned by a military judge pending an investigation into charges of espionage. (CPJ)

On 11 June three French journalists from the *Courrier des Balkans* electronic newsletter were detained and questioned for eight hours in a local shop in Montenegro by military officials. **Philippe Mirkovic**, **Laurent Rouy** and **Jean-Arnault Derens** were then transported by military escort to military barracks, where they were again interrogated. The journalists were released the next day. (CPJ)

Koha Ditore, the largest and most influential Albanian-language newspaper in Kosovo, resumed distribution in Albania and Kosovo on 15 June with the news that publisher **Veton Surroi**, and the editor of its English edition, **Dukagjin Gorani**, were safe in Prishtina. Surroi, a member of the Albanian delegation to aborted Rambouillet peace talks, was placed under the protection of

NATO forces. On 24 March, police shot and killed the guard at the newspaper's office in Prishtina. *Koha Ditore* then relocated to Macedonia under control of its editor **Baton Haixhu** to recommence publication on 22 April (*Index* 4/1999). (Greek Helsinki Monitor)

The body of **Senol Alit**, an Albanian from Macedonia acting as the interpreter for the two German journalists **Volker Kraemer** and **Gabriel Gruener** shot by Serbian forces (*Index* 4/1999), was found on 15 June by German soldiers near the car in which they were travelling. Previously NATO troops had been kept away from the vehicle by Serbian soldiers. (CPJ, IFJ)

Owner of Kikinda-based stations Radio Senta and VK Radio, **Zoran Malesevic**, appeared in court on 15 June on misdemeanour charges filed against him by the telecommunications ministry (*Index* 3/1999). The ministry claimed Malesevic had been operating radio stations without a licence, despite the fact that the ministry was obliged to issue licences after collecting fees for the use of the frequencies on which Radio Senta and VK Radio broadcast. (Association of Independent Electronic Media)

Two British journalists came under fire in Kosovo on 17 June when their car was ambushed from the roadside after an unidentified man bearing a gun attempted to flag them down. *Daily Record* reporter **Simon Houston** and photographer **Chris Watt** were shot during the ambush, both receiving superficial head wounds. Their Albanian interpreter **Xherdat Shabani** was shot in the shoulder. The gunmen were not wearing uniforms of any kind and could have been attempting to steal the car, which bore no press markings and had Macedonian number plates. (CPJ, Press Association)

SIERRA LEONE

Four journalists from the Freetown-based *Independent Observer* were arrested by ECOMOG peacekeepers following a raid on the paper's office in early June. Editor **Sorie Sudan Sesay** and administrative manager **Bai Bai Sesay** were detained, as were the deputy editor of the *Progress* newspaper, **Jerry Tryson** and reporter **Ibrahim Sorie** after ECOMOG troops discovered weapons at the office. Eyewitnesses claim that ECOMOG planted them. Staff were also beaten and equipment seized. The *Independent Observer*'s managing editor, **Jonathan Leigh**, had been arrested on 17 May but was subsequently released (*Index* 4/1999). (RSF)

Gibril Foday Musa, editor of the *New Tablet*, was assaulted and detained on 10 June by the Kamajor civil militia. They were looking for the editor of the *New Sierra Leonean*, with which the *New Tablet* shares offices but, unable to find him, seized upon Musa and the building's caretaker. The raid followed an article in the *New Sierra Leonean* alleging that Kamajor forces intended to topple President Ahmad Tejan Kabbah. (RSF)

Twenty journalists taking refuge in Guinea allege that Revolutionary United Front (RUF) rebels targeted journalists for execution during the fighting in January when over 10 were murdered and many more imprisoned (*Index* 2/1999). The claim followed a meeting with RSF officials on 15 June. (RSF)

Journalist **Abdul Rhaman Swaray**, a reporter with the *Independent Observer*, was arrested on 1 July by policemen from the Special Security Department after the publication of his article alleging 300 RUF rebels had joined the regular army. (RSF)

A number of journalists thought either to have been killed or captured in the January fighting have since re-emerged, according to a report on 22 July. **Christopher Coker**, **Momodu Adams**, **Maada Maaka Swarray** and **Chernon Ojuku Sesay** had all returned to Freetown by July. Unlike the first two, who were held by the rebels, Swarray, who worked for the Sierra Leone Broadcasting Service (SLBS), and Sesay, editor of the *Pool* newspaper, had been in hiding from the security forces of President Tejan Kabbah who sought them on charges of collaborating with the Armed Forces Ruling Council (AFRC). (RSF)

Four journalists sentenced to death for collaborating with the AFRC military junta – **Jipo Felix George**, **Dennis Ayodele Smith**, **Mildred Hancilles** and **Ibrahim Ben Kargbo** – were released after spending 200 days in jail,

according to a 29 July report (*Index* 6/1999). George was director-general of the SLBS and Smith the programming director, Hancilles was a SLBS journalist and Kargbo editor-in-chief of the *New Citizen*, one of the country's oldest independent newspapers. The journalists had always declared their innocence. (RSF)

Four journalists were among a group of people taken hostage by former military junta rebels on 4 August in the Okra Hills some 40 miles east of Freetown. Reuters reporter **Christo Johnson**, **Pasco Temple**, a journalist with Liberia's Star Radio, **Ade Campbell** of SLBS radio and **Chernor Bangura**, a cameraman for SLBS television had accompanied UN military observers and aid workers to witness the handover of about 200 children abducted by the rebels during the eight-year civil war. (CPJ)

SOMALIA

Journalists **Abulkadir Ali** and **Mohamed Deeq** of *Sahan* newspaper, and **Ahmed Mohamed Ali** of *Riyaq*, were arrested on 2 August by authorities in the unrecognised 'Puntland Republic'. The three are well known for expressing their opinions on the regional authorities (RSF)

SRI LANKA

On 15 July over a dozen members of the media were physically assaulted and had their equipment taken by police and military personnel while covering a political rally of the opposition United National

Party (UNP) in Colombo. (Free Media Movement, *Sunday Observer, Sunday Leader*)

Srilal Priyantha, a journalist for the Sinhalese-language *Lakbima*, was reported in mid-July to have undergone surgery to his genitalia following injuries received while being tortured by members of the Criminal Investigation Department. Priyantha was arrested in May on murder charges, but his colleagues believe that the government is trying to divert attention from the stories of military corruption he uncovered as a journalist (*Index* 3/1999, 4/1999). (Asian Human Rights Commission)

On 29 July **Neelan Tiruchelvam**, a widely respected lawyer, academic, human rights activist and moderate Tamil Member of Parliament, was killed in a suicide bomb attack in Colombo. Thiruchelvam, who was also Chair of the London-based Minority Rights Group and one of the principal architects of President Kumaratunga's constitutional proposals to end the country's brutal civil war, was apparently killed by the separatist Liberation Tigers of Tamil Eelam (LTTE). (India Abroad News Service, *Independent*, AI, A19, Asian Human Rights Commission, *Sunday Observer*)

Recent Publications: *Reaping The Whirlwind: Ethnic Conflict, Ethnic Politics in Sri Lanka* by K. M. de Silva (Penguin, 1998, pp 388); *Gaps in the Krishanthy Kumarasamy Case: Disappearances & Accountability – Special Report No. 12* (UTHR-J, April 1999)

SUDAN

On 5 July the government suspended the publication of the independent daily *Al Rai Al-Akhar* for five days as a punishment for publishing articles critical of the government. Two other newspapers were also suspended on 5 July for two days for publishing information on alleged embezzlement by a government official. (RSF)

SWEDEN

On 28 June **Peter Karlson**, a freelance journalist, was injured with his young son when a car bomb went off outside their home in Stockholm. Karlson specialises in covering extreme right-wing movements. (RSF)

SYRIA

On 29 June the authorities faxed the London-based daily *Al-Quds al-'Arabi* to say that the newspaper could no longer be distributed in the state. Though no reason was given, it is believed the move is a response to a 28 June article by editor-in-chief **Abdel Barri Atwan,** which criticised government inaction in Israel's 24 May-5 June bombing of Lebanon. For three months prior to the ban, censors removed page 13 of *Al-Quds al-'Arabi* before distributing it. It is presumed that the serialisation of the previously unpublished memoirs of **Akram al-Hourani**, one-time deputy to Egypt's President Gamal Nasser, was the reason for the censorship. (*Al-Quds al-'Arabi*, RSF)

TAJIKISTAN

The exposure of drug-running gangs by Lieutenant-Colonel **Djumakhon Hotami** on his weekly television programme on crime and corruption seems the most likely reason for his 4 July murder. Hotami was killed near his home by attackers firing at point-blank range. (RFE/RL)

TANZANIA

The *Majira* newspaper was banned on 22 July after it misreported proposals to raise the salaries and perks of government regional ministers to about US$11,000 a month and those of regional commissioners to US$10,000. The amounts quoted were unfortunately for annual not monthly stipends. Despite the editor **Jesse Kweyu**'s apology, the government maintained the ban until 30 July. (Media Institute of Southern Africa)

THAILAND

On 15 July the private secretary of deputy prime minister Trairong Suwankhiri and seven armed men entered the offices of the *Thai Post* and demanded a printed correction to a story that alleged that Trairong had avoided a dialogue with protesting fishermen in Trang province because he was afraid of the so-called 'mob'. His private secretary, Chalie Noppawong, na Ayuthaya threatened to 'come back, but in a different manner' if the *Post* printed any more unflattering articles about his boss. (Reporters Association of Thailand, Southeast Asian Press Alliance, CPJ)

TOGO

On 29 June editor-in-chief of the newspaper *Le Reporter des Temps Nouveaux*, **Romain Koudjdji**, was released from detention following the conclusion of his trial in which he received a fine of one million CFA francs (US$1,562) and an additional symbolic fine of 1 CFA franc payable to the police department. (IFJ)

TURKEY

The Radio and Television Supreme Board (RTUK) closed down the private radio station, Umut Radyo (Radio Hope) of Istanbul for 15 days, it was reported on 5 June, for 'violating broadcast principles'. The RTUK also ordered the closure of TV channels Kent TV for three days, Show TV for two days, ATV, SKY TV and As TV for one day each. (*Radikal*)

Hasan Deniz, editor-in-chief of the daily *Ozgur Bakis*, was remanded by Istanbul State Security Court on 4 June for a news story published in the 47th issue of the paper. **Vedat Cetin**, who was prosecuted at Istanbul SSC in connection with his article 'Kadinlar da Ozgurlesmeli' ('Women Should Be Free'), published in the banned daily *Gundem*, was sentenced to over a year in prison and fined. The journal *Mucadele Birligi* was also closed for one month in June and a member of staff at the Adana office of the daily *Ozgur Halk* was detained in Urfa on 4 June. (*Ozgur Bakis*,TIHV)

Lale Turuc, Adana representative of the journal *Alinterimiz*, and a colleague named **Nihal Gul**, were detained by soldiers outside Ceyhan prison on 8 June. (*Evrensel*, TIHV)

The trial against **Cezmi Yalcinkaya, Beyaz Emektar** and **Nuri Turan**, all members of the Izmir branch of the Mesopotamian Cultural Centre (MKM) (*Index* 4/1999), was concluded on 10 June. They were each sentenced to a year in prison for singing songs in Kurdish at a Youth festival. (*Ozgur Bakis*,TIHV)

Vedat Bakir, news director of Radyo Karacadag (*Index* 2/1998) in Urfa, was imprisoned on 7 July by Diyarbakir State Security Court in connection with a speech he had made on the closed-down Kurdish satellite channel, Med-TV. He received a sentence of 20 months. (*Ozgur Bakis*,TIHV)

The Izmir governorate banned the Izmir branch of the Human Rights Association from distributing bulletins and hanging placards in the city in support of the Campaign for Freedom of Thought on 14 June. They cited the 'existing situation in the country' as grounds for the ban. (*Ozgur Bakis*,TIHV)

Istanbul SSC closed down the journal *Uzun Yuruys* (The Long Walk) for a month on 14 June for an article entitled 'The panorama of the region and the Kurds'. (*Ozgur Bakis*, TIHV)

Andrew Finkel, correspondent for *Time*, *The Times,* the Turkish daily *Sabah* and CNN TV, went on trial on 11 June for his article

'Sirnak 1998'. He is charged with insulting the military and faces up to six months in prison. The trial was postponed so that the article could be reviewed by a panel of experts. (RSF, *Sabah*,TIHV)

Police raided the head office of the journal *Partizan* in Istanbul on 14 June, detaining editor-in-chief **Nuran Baskan**, along with staff members **Kemal Tohumlu** and **Servet Ciracioglu**. (*Evrensel*, TIHV)

Police in Ankara raided the main office of the journal *Furkan*, said to be the publication of the radical Islamic IBDA-C organisation, and detained three people on June 15, while in Istanbul the 135th issue of the journal *Partizan* was confiscated for unspecified articles. (*Ozgur Bakis*, TIHV)

Two journalists with the pro-Kurdish weekly *Hevi* were detained in the state of emergency region on 15 June and reportedly tortured. **Mehmet Eren** and **Aydogan Inal** were taken to Diyarbakir security headquarters and questioned about the newspaper and banned organisations. Eren was blindfolded, stripped and beaten. He was taken to an isolated place and threatened with death if he did not leave the city. (RSF)

Faik Bulut, journalist with *Halkin Gunlugu*, was arrested at the headquarters of the private television station ATV on 18 June. He was due to appear in a live programme but was detained for articles published in the journal. (*Cumhuriyet*, *Evrensel*, TIHV)

Journalists covering President Suleyman Demirel's visit to the Istanbul Metropolitan Municipality on 21 June were harassed and blocked by police. **Kemal Diyarbekir**, reporter for the Turkish daily *Hurriyet*, was jostled and his press card seized, while a driver for Show TV, **Ertugrul Kindem**, was beaten up by security police outside. (*Ozgur Baki*, TIHV)

Huseyin Aykol, journalist with the foreign service of the pro-Kurd daily *Ozgur Bakis*, was arrested on 18 June at Istanbul airport as she was about to leave for the Netherlands. The police checked whether the publications she had on her were banned and confiscated one edition of her newspaper and a few books. She was released after being questioned for one day. (RSF)

Abdullah Gunduz, owner of Aram publishing house, was detained on 24 June on separatist charges for his book *Gunesimizi Karatamazsiniz*. **Nuray Yazar**, editor-in-chief of the newspaper *Proleter Halkin Birligi* (Proletarian People's Union), was remanded in custody on 25 June when the paper was closed down for 15 days. (*Ozgur Bakis*, TIHV)

Amberin Zaman, correspondent for the US daily *Washington Post* and the Voice of America, was arrested by plainclothes police on 28 June in the southeastern city of Mardin. She was made to strip to her underwear and her notes and cellphone were confiscated. She was released after making contact with the US embassy. (RSF)

On 4 July a German TV crew from ZDF were attacked in Ankara and accused of pro-PKK propaganda. **Manfred Bainczyk**, head of the Turkish office, **Jurgen Heck**, cameraman and **Manfred Peter**, assistant cameraman, were arrested by police while covering the visit of a German member of the Green party, Claudia Roth. (RSF)

The European Court for Human Rights found Turkey guilty in 15 separate cases on 8 July: 11 times for violations of the freedom of expression of Kurds; nine times for violation of the right to be tried by an independent court; and two cases where Kurds had been tortured and killed. Thirteen petitions were filed by journalists, lawyers, trade unionists, writers or academics who had been sentenced to imprisonment and fines for having published, or allowed to be published, remarks favourable to the Kurdish cause. They included journalist **Haluk Gerger** (*Index* 1/1995, 5/1995, 6/1995, 1/1996, 5/1998, 6/1998) professor **Fikret Baskaya**, union president **Munir Ceylan** and publisher **Kamil Tekin**. (*Cildekt No 138*)

It was reported on 10 July that **Zeynel Engin**, owner and editor-in-chief of the fortnightly *Halkin Gunlugu* (People's Diary), was sentenced to 16 months' imprisonment and a fine of over TL2 billion (approx US$2,000) for articles in the publication. (RSF)

Sixteen members of the People's Democracy Party (HADEP), including the President **Murat Bozlak**, who had been charged with giving assistance to a terrorist organisation, were released on 12 July by the State Security Court in Ankara (*Index* 1/1999). It was judged that there were no grounds for prolonging their incarceration. (*Cildekt No 138*)

On 4 August the minister of justice proposed a bill to give amnesty to up to 40,000 prisoners. The amnesty will apply to common law and financial crimes, but not to 'prisoners of criminal thought', such as **Leyla Zana** (*Index*, 1/1997, 6/1998, 4/1999), **Ismail Besikci**, **Akin Birdal** (*Index* 4/1998, 5/1998, 1/1999, 4/1999) and other intellectuals in jail for 'crimes against the State'. (*Cildekt No 140*)

Turkey's musician of the year for 1998, **Ahmet Kaya**, who faces a 10-year prison sentence for having said publicly that he wanted to compose songs in Kurdish, went on trial on 25 August. His lawyers accuse the press of a 'media lynching campaign' against the singer, with a rash of libellous articles in recent weeks. (*Cildekt No 140*)

Parliamentary authorities erased a reference to Kurdish as a second language from the official biography of an Islamist MP, it was reported on 5 August. **Mehmet Fuat Firat** listed Kurdish as one of his foreign languages, but deputies complained that Kurdish is not a recognised language in Turkey. A Kurdish newspaper protested at Firat's having to list Kurdish as a foreign language when it was, in fact, his mother tongue. (Reuters)

UKRAINE

On 26 July the broadcasts of four non-governmental Crimean TV companies – Chernomorskaya TV, Simferopol City ITV, Ekran TV and Kerch TV – were stopped following allegations that the channels were not granted permits to broadcast on the frequency channels of the Crimea TV and Radio Broadcasting Centre. The move comes just months before the 31 October presidential elections. (GDF, CPJ)

UNITED KINGDOM

On 9 June Liverpool pensioner **George Staunton**, 78, was arrested and charged with racially aggravated criminal damage for writing the slogans 'Don't Forget the 1945 War' and 'Free Speech for England', across a wall during the European Parliamentary elections. Staunton had been putting up posters for the UK Independence Party. Police interpreted the graffiti as racist, but Staunton defended himself as a patriot. (*Daily Telegraph*)

On 8 July five law lords unanimously overturned an appeal court ruling that the ban on prison inmates' media visits was justified. They also said that the refusal on the part of prison governors to allow journalists to interview inmates, unless they agreed not to write about the stories, was unlawful. The appeal was brought by two convicted murderers **Michael O'Brien**, now out on bail pending a new appeal and **Ian Simms**, who is serving a life sentence for murder in Long

Lartin prison. (*Guardian*)

On 12 July the General Synod of the Church of England agreed to introduce trial by a closed tribunal of clergy who 'err on doctrine'. The bishop's proposal includes offences against 'doctrine, ritual and ceremonial' matters. (*Daily Telegraph*)

On 15 July Channel 4 News reported that the UK's eavesdropping facility, the Government Communications Headquarters (GCHQ) in Cheltenham, had intercepted all Irish international communications to the UK since the late 1980s via a 45m tower in Capenhurst, Cheshire. Allegedly set up to spy on terrorist organisations in Ireland, the communication tower may have been used for listening to Irish politicians and gathering information of economic and commercial significance. When the £20 million tower was built in 1988, the Ministry of Defence allegedly offered Capenhurst residents free fencing and double-glazing if they agreed to not discuss the site. (*Independent, Guardian, Irish Times*)

On 23 July **Alison Redmond-Bate**, an evangelical preacher for the Leeds-based fundamentalist group Faith Ministries, appealed to the high court when her conviction for 'obstructing a police officer in the course of his duty' was upheld. Redmond-Bate was preaching on the steps of Wakefield cathedral with her mother and another woman when people began telling them to shut up. Fearing a breach of

the peace, the police officer asked the women to stop. Redmond-Bate continued to preach. (*Guardian*)

On 19 July Radio 1 rap disc jockey **Tim Westwood** was shot in Kennington, South London while travelling by car from a music festival. Westwood is one of the few white DJs to concentrate on black rap and hip-hop music. It is thought that the shooting may be linked to others in the London area by 'Yardie' Jamaican gangsters. (*Daily Telegraph*)

On 19 July government published plans to lock up psychopaths indefinitely, even if they have not committed a crime. People who are seen to be 'dangerous, severely mentally disordered' would be held in prison, hospital or in specially-designed units indefinitely. (BBC News On-line, *Daily Telegraph*)

On 28 July the Appeal Court in London ruled that 17 soldiers should be granted anonymity when giving evidence to the 'Bloody Sunday' inquiry. Relatives of those who died have suggested that 'the independence of the inquiry has been undermined by this ruling because it has clouded [its] openness and transparency.' (*Irish Times*)

In July the Arts Council of Northern Ireland withheld a grant of £18,000 for the drama *Forced Upon Us*, which had been playing to packed houses at the West Belfast Festival. The play, a joint production between the Dubbeljoint theatre company and a West Belfast community

An Open Letter To Members of the Board of the Pacifica and Mary Frances Berry, Chair

Your administration's actions in locking out union workers, community volunteers and the hundreds of people who regularly use KPFA to speak out on social, political and artistic causes has proven intolerable to the community which supports and depends on the station.

Your administration's use of armed guards and anti-labour consultants, its insistence on the arrest and prosecution of more than 100 non-violent staff and protesters, its imposition of a 'gag order' to silence those who speak their conscience, or even to report on the crisis, is antithetical to the network's mission.

You have made your board self-appointing and impervious to outside input.

You have recklessly squandered the contributions of KPFA's donors on security and public relations firms. Intentionally or not, you have done what decades of right-wing attacks failed to accomplish: you have weakened Pacifica to the point of collapse.

We the undersigned academics, elected officials, labour leaders, artists, writers and activists find these actions and events both reprehensible and ominous in light of the rapid monopolisation of mass media. We demand that all staff fired in the present crisis be reinstated, that censorship throughout the Pacifica network be lifted, that donor funds be accounted for and that democratic governance be instituted in a network founded 50 years ago to encourage open discussion and active participation by those whom it serves. ❏

This edited text was published in the New York Times *on 18 August in response to the armed removal from KPFA of host Dennis Bernstein on 13 July for discussing on-air the ongoing dispute between staff and management about the future direction of one of the US' oldest subscriber radio stations. KPFA was founded by the late pacifist journalist Lewis Hill in 1949 with the specific aim of providing airtime to the individual commentator. Alice Walker, Angela Davies, Joan Baez, Lawrence Ferlinghetti, Noam Chomsky and Pete Seeger were among nearly 100 US artists, intellectuals and labour leaders to sign the letter.*

drama group, JustUs, was described by the external assessor as 'clumsy propaganda'. It contained the rape of a Catholic woman by a Protestant man and was co-written by **Christine Poland** and former IRA prisoner **Brenda Murphy**. *(Irish Times)*

USA

On 3 June a Federal District Court in Richmond, Virginia, ordered the Surrey County School Board to allow **Kent McNew** to return to school. The high-school sophomore had been suspended on 28 April for coming to school with his hair dyed blue. (American Civil Liberties Union)

The mother of an 11-year-old has filed suit against Toys R Us after she heard a talking Austin Powers doll say: 'Do I make you horny baby, do I?' during her shopping trip. (*The Times*)

On 9 July a federal judge ruled that the Missouri city of Republic must remove the *ichtheus*, a Christian symbol, from its logo. 'The Republic city seal pervasively invades the daily lives of non-Christians and sends a message that they are outsiders,' he was quoted as saying. (American Civil Liberties Union)

On 19 July Judge Jerry Buchmayer ordered the city of Wichita Falls to place *Heather Has Two Mommies* and *Daddy's Roommate* back in the youth non-fiction area of the public library. The books were moved to an adult area of the library under a resolution adopted in February. (American Civil

Liberties Union)

On 27 July the owners of the *New England Journal of Medicine* dismissed editor in chief **Dr. Jerome Kassirer** after he balked at using the journal's prestige to sell unrelated publications and products. (*International Herald Tribune*)

UZBEKISTAN

Reports on 18 June said that Tashkent police had detained 25 boys aged between 9 and 12 for allegedly distributing leaflets promulgating fundamentalist Islam and calling for the overthrow of President Islam Karimov. (Associated Press, Interfax)

It was reported on 25 June that **Akhmadkhon Turakhanov**, a member of the unregistered Independent Human Rights Organisation of Uzbekistan (NOPCHU), had died in prison, apparently from untreated diabetes and tuberculosis. In March, Turakhanov was sentenced to five years in jail for 'hooliganism and sedition'. Also on 25 June, NOPCHU chairman **Mikhail Ardzinov** was detained on his way to observe a trial of alleged Islamic subversives and beaten over a period of 14 hours by officers of the Tashkent City Department of Internal Affairs (GUVD). Ardzinov was taken for medical attention at the US Embassy, where the examination revealed two broken ribs, concussion and contused kidneys. On 10 July, NOPCHU member **Ismail Adylov** was detained at his home by Internal Affairs Ministry (MVD) officers. Four days later a Tashkent court

handed down a five-year sentence for fraud and harbouring a criminal to **Mahbuba Kasymova** who, like Adylov, had belonged to both NOPCHU and the banned Birlik Democratic Party. Kasymova was arrested in April and portrayed on state television shortly afterwards as a 'criminal'. Her trial lasted three hours. (AI, HRW, RFE/RL)

On 28 June a Tashkent court sentenced six men to death and 14 others to terms of between 10 and 20 years for causing the 16 February 1999 explosions in Tashkent that killed 16 people and injured 128. The 22 convictions represent just the first of several prosecutions of alleged Islamic terrorists. Six of the 22 (including at least one sentenced to death) were in already in custody or jail at the time of the blasts. Hundreds of the defendants' supporters were arrested for distributing leaflets in Tashkent during the trial. (Agence France-Presse)

Speaking on Iranian Radio's Uzbek Service on 24 July, **Mohammad Solih**, the leader of the banned Erk Democratic Party, denied government charges that he funded the dissemination of subversive literature and was involved in the 16 February bombings. (RFE/RL)

Three Christians working for the Full Gospel Church in Nukus, capital of the Karakalpak Autonomous Republic, have been jailed for long periods, the Keston Institute reported on 23 July. All three were convicted of possessing drugs, but both they and their supporters say the drugs were planted on them by police. One was also convicted of illegal religious activities. (RFE/RL)

VIETNAM

Prominent Vietnam dissident **Nguyen Thanh Giang** (*Index* 3/1999, 4/1999), who was charged on 13 April for violating Penal Code 205, has been forced to report his activities to police officials once a week, after ending the second of his six-day hunger strikes in protest against his treatment. Nguyen, who has not been given a formal date for his trial, was arrested after being detained with anti-communist documents. The geophysicist is restricted from leaving Hanoi without permission. On 15 July a fellow dissident, **General Tran Do**, with whom Nguyen had been in telephone contact, was refused permission to publish a newspaper by the general secretary of the Communist party, Le Kha Phieu. (Reuters/RSF)

YEMEN

On 4 August the Seera Court of First Instance sentenced **Hisham Basharaheel**, editor of the thrice-weekly *Al-Ayyam*, and **Ali Haitham Ghareeb**, a reporter with the paper, to suspended prison terms of six and 10 months, respectively, on charges that included 'instigating national feuds', 'instigating the spirit of separatism' and 'harming national unity'. The charges were filed in May in response to an article written by Ghareeb published in the 27 February edition, entitled 'Let's Talk About Unity from the Social Perspective'. Basharaheel was additionally charged with violating a January court order banning publication of court proceedings from the trial of a group of UK nationals who were then facing terrorism charges in Aden. The article, published on 3 March and titled 'Lawyer Hmeidan Calls for Dismissal of Trial of Her British Clients on Account of Improper Legal Proceedings', summarised a story by the BBC which reported that the lawyer for the eight men had urged that their cases be dismissed on procedural grounds. It is unclear whether Basharaheel was convicted of this charge, since the court did not release details of the judgement. The judge ruled against the prosecution's request that *Al-Ayyam* be closed indefinitely. (CPJ)

ZIMBABWE

A report carried in the *Financial Gazette* newspaper said that President Robert Mugabe had written to parliament on 8 and 9 June advising the speaker that he was withholding his assent of the new Public Order and Security Bill (POSB) because of 'inadequacies' insofar as it dealt with the media, particularly in regards to the publication of 'stories pertaining to the security of the country'. The POSB was approved by parliament last year and was meant to replace the draconian Law and Order Maintenance Act, a law that was enacted two decades before independence. Media reports in April said that the president had in fact signed the bill, although there was no clarity on when it would be enacted. This is the first time that Mugabe has refused to sign a bill already approved by parliament. (Media Institute of Southern Africa)

Compiled by: Jake Barnes, John Kamau, Daniel Rogers (Africa); Rupert Clayton, Andrew Kendle, Alex Lockwood, Jon Parr (Asia); Alex Lockwood, (eastern Europe and CIS); Brydie Bethell, Daniel Rogers (south and central America); Arif Azad, Gill Newsham, Neil Sammonds (Middle East); Billie Felix Jeyes (north America and Pacific); Catherine Jackson (UK and western Europe).

The walls remain

The wall that straddled Berlin from 1961 to 1989 was a powerful symbol of a city divided against itself. And more: it stood for the separation of peoples and ideologies worldwide. Its fall in 1989 did not bring down those walls that continue to separate nations and cities.

'O wicked wall, through whom I see no bliss!
Cursed be thy stones for thus deceiving me!'
William Shakespeare, *A Midsummer Night's Dream*

Graffiti artist Menager's Petit Homme Blanc, Great Wall of China, 1989 – Credit: Menager/Rex

Whose city? Jerusalem's wall – Credit: Rex

Face to the wall. Russian execution – Credit: Rex

The 'Green Line' that divides Cyprus – Credit: Adrian Brooks/Rex

Belfast 31 August 1994: eve of a shaky ceasfire – Credit: Crispin Rodwell/Rex

End of the Wall — Credit: Alfred/Rex

NADIRE MATER

Soldiers' tales

Mehmedin Kitab (*Mehmed's Book*) by Nadire Mater is the
story of life in the Turkish army on the southeastern front
as told by 42 of the 220,000 conscripts who have fought for
their country in its civil war against the Kurds. On 23 June this
year *Mehmedin Kitab: soldiers who have fought in the
Southeast speak out*, to give it its full title, was banned by an
Istanbul court on charges of 'insulting and belittling the
military'. The court also ordered the seizure of all existing
copies.

The military took its time: the book had been around since
April and was already in its fourth reprint when it made its
views known. Maybe it was the prospect of an English-language
translation, already delivered to an editor with a view to UK or
US publication, that alarmed the sclerotic generals who still
rule Turkey.

This is undoubtedly one of the most important and explosive
books to come out of Turkey in the last decade. The soldiers'
testimony exposes the army, the politicians and makes it clear
that this is an 'unnecessary' and 'unjust' war that is driving the
country to bankrupcy and political suicide. 'I fear we are
storing up the wrath to come,' says one of the '*Mehmets*' – a
generic term for the conscript squaddies

FISHY BUSINESS

I wanted to go southeast. I'd heard a lot about the war there and I
was curious. I was in tears by the first day: my head was shaved and the
way your seniors and the officers treat you demolishes every shred of
self–confidence.

After three months I went on leave, and then to another training
centre in the Umraniye district of Istanbul. Eventually, half the battalion

Peace activist confronts Turkish soldier near Diyabakir – Credit: Julia Guest

was sent southeast, to Siirt province, by train with loads of ammunition.
Night travel was forbidden. We stopped at night and went on in the
morning. It took almost a week and we were scared. The track was long
and exposed to attack. In Kurtalan we left the train and were transported
to the Siirt infantry battalion headquarters on trucks. We are going to
establish a military post in Guclukonak.

As soon as we arrive we are ordered to detect land mines with
detectors. There are a lot of mines – anti-personnel mines, anti-vehicle
mines – and the soldiers are frightened, unable to move back or forward.
The detectors don't always work. Some of them can't detect plastic
mines, others detect any kind of mines and others buzz even if there's no

Turkish troops block European peace activists from entering Diyabakir – Credit: Julia Guest

mine; they are simply out of order.

The villagers like the infantry. An old man complains: 'The gendarmes strike, the special teams strike, and the PKK comes and strikes condemning us as traitors, spies.' Then he asks: 'Tell us, commander, on whom should we rely, what should we do?' It was there

I came to understand the mistakes of the guerrillas and of the state that insists on continuing the war.

There was a canteen, the profits from which went to the major in charge of the battalion; one can of cola sells for US$2. Soldiers can't afford a cola a day on their salaries. High quality (Dardanelles brand) canned fish is provided for the soldiers by the state. But at the front the rank and file never see it; it's saved for the officers. Soldiers are only worth unbranded canned food. I used to escape from the guards, sneak into the warehouse, steal the canned fish and distribute it to the soldiers. They needed it; it has more calories.

Once we were searching for mines on the road to Guclukonak. A vehicle passes over a mine and the car is demolished, but there are no casualties. At that moment an old couple from the village appear; they are going to hospital on foot. One of the soldiers gets out of the car and shoots straight at the man. He is killed. We were taking a rest at that point but we heard the bang and went there. The old woman was crying. A nervous soldier would often shoot for no reason, without warning. We were not searching villages; most had already been evacuated. Where there were still people we were razing the village. We even burned down mosques. We'd surround a village and our commander would order the villagers to evacuate it. Three teams go in, people are forced out of their homes. The houses are searched. Men, women and children are separated from each other. The men are denounced: 'You will leave this place, you support the PKK, you give them food.' The people are helpless; they take their belongings and the teams rush into the houses, douse them with petrol and set them alight. We watch the flames of the burning village from the top of the hills.

I have seen all I wanted to know; my curiosity is satisfied. I have my answer. My impression is that the state wants the war to continue. If it met the people's demands, responded to their cultural, linguistic and ethnic needs, and improved their conditions, there would be no reason to make war. Before my military service I was curious about the enemy. Now I have answered all the questions. Who is my enemy? The ruling classes. Who else could it be?

I have not encountered the PKK as such. In the past, I used to call them the 'PKK', but after everything I've seen I call them 'guerrillas'. I believe the state is carrying on an unjust war there. I was not especially interested in the Kurds. For me they are no different from others in our country – Pontians, Circassians, Armenians. Before going for military service I used to read *Ozgur Gundem*, the pro-Kurdish newspaper. I knew they were a party to the conflict. But it was the only paper reporting on the war zone. Others would simply report 'there has been a clash and XX men have been killed'.

One day they brought an old man along with his two mules. They had caught him with two sacks of flour and were accusing him of taking them to the PKK. They were dragging him along the ground at the end of a rope. I guess he was around 60. But it's difficult to tell: people there are so ground down even the young look old. The man was crying and shouting, denying the charge.

I never believed the 'Guclukonak incident' was the guerrillas' work. In January 1996 11 people from Guclukonak village, mostly village guards, were found burned to death in a van. Although the military accused the PKK, independent investigators and journalists had proof that there was no guerrilla activity in the vicinity at the time, and that the victims were in conflict with the local military authorities over their refusal to join the village guard system.

Down there you are fighting scores of wars. Psychologically you are fighting against yourself as well as your adversary. Whether you actually take part in a conflict or not, you are a part of it; you have to protect yourself. If you don't want to harm them, you are believed to be on the other side. And there is the fight to get the good quality canned fish. The toughest of all the wars you fight is against your own presence there against your will: your civil war against yourself.

When I was back in my hometown, Tonya, people expected me to tell them what was going on down there. I told them everything: what the PKK was doing, what we were doing, how the villages were being evacuated, how the war was being conducted. I have changed. I have a much clearer idea of who is responsible for the war, who benefits from it. The regular officers want the war to continue; they make a lot of money. Because it's risky and those that go beyond the call of duty are certain to get killed, they wouldn't join us on ambushes but sent their juniors – national service officers are always put with the rank and file, they're like friends.

ONE UNDER THE FLAG

Back in town, after I was demobbed, I saw terrorists everywhere. Out there, civilians were either terrorists or their supporters. There are good people, of course, but you never see them, you never go downtown. You are up on the mountains. And when you do get away from there and come back among normal people, they are all PKK to you. I feel stupid. I keep looking around as if someone might shoot me. When I see a mountain, I think, 'there's a terrorist there, targeting me'. I go out to the country and see a terrorist behind every rock. Sometimes I throw myself on the ground, take up a position.

Three months after demob I was riding a bike when there was a sudden flash of lightening and I threw myself on the ground: I had mistaken the thunder for gunfire. People around laughed at me. I got up and I, too, started to laugh at myself. In the day, I imagine I am still at the front, but the night is much worse. When I feel a bit depressed my mind is filled with crazy notions. I think to myself: 'All these people are terrorists, I should take my gun and kill them'

Until I did military service I had never seen a dead body. There I saw every kind of killing – torture, burning, all sorts. It wouldn't bother me if they carved a man with a razor right in front of me: I have become a stone.

Last night in my dream we were fighting, my buddies were falling beside me. When you hunt partridge on the mountains they are exterminated; when you hunt the female of the species it cannot reproduce. The same goes for terrorists. Put a guard on every spring. They can stand hunger but not thirst. When they come to the springs for water shoot them, poison the water, whatever.

Today the terrorist goes to the village, and tortures the newborn baby to death, but when he is taken prisoner he is fed by the state. What kind of human right is this? Where are the rights of his victims? I recognise no human rights. My right is my weapon. I protect myself with that. The man in charge orders you to march on the mountains. If you're killed you're a martyr. You protect your own rights.

It was a terrible life on the mountains but I am still proud of it. Now I have a good job, but if I were called up this moment, I'd drop everything and join the army. When I watch the TV news from there I yearn to be back among them. There you are fighting for your country and your nation.

I applied to join the special teams [regulars] but you have to be at least a high-school graduate. Primary-school graduates can become MPs but a peasant's son can't join the special teams because he's only a primary-school graduate. In the southeast none of the soldiers are the sons of the rich. Lots of rich boys were appointed to my unit but they lasted only 24 hours.

All power is in the hands of the military; it's our heroic armed forces who are fighting terrorism. Deputies are afraid to visit the war zone to take a look; they even go to the mosque with 10 bodyguards. Man, this is the house of the God. God will protect you.

You fight for the nation but you are not worth a penny. 'You've not fought for me, you've fought for the country,' say politicians. And the state doesn't give a damn either. Inequality reigns supreme in this country: the scales are weighted on the side of the wealthy.

After my demob I went to the war zone to visit my friends the village guards [government-appointed militias]. They blame the state. They have land but they can't sow it. They give bread to the terrorists at night and to the soldiers in the morning. They live with death.

All Muslims are brothers. A handful of men from a whole people fights for the PKK and all Kurds pay. They are denied jobs and discriminated against. I want an end to discrimination: no Turkism no Kurdism. I want equality. These people should be educated, jobs should be created for them. The region should be given the same development opportunities as the western parts of the country. Nature is so beautiful there the region could be developed for tourism. All should feel themselves Turkish citizens under the Turkish flag and speak the Turkish language. All should live in a world of equals.

NOW I KNOW I'M A KURD

I was based 45 kilometres from my birthplace. This is state policy: we people from the southeast are made to confront each other.

These people are terribly oppressed. Once we fought a battle on the Tendurek Mountains. We killed 16 PKK. We lined them up on the ground. When we got up in the morning their ears had gone. The rightists had cut their ears off during the night watch. I felt terribly bad; I had never seen corpses torn like these. The battalion commander was very angry. He asked if there were any *imams* among us. A few raised their hands. He called them and asked: 'Tell us if what they have done is justified? Even if they are enemies, harming the dead is a sin in our religion.'

I was stretching out on the bed later when I saw him; he was enclosing an ear in his letter to their family. If I'd objected, he might well have accused me of 'supporting the separatists'. Then I'd probably have been charged with 'being a member of the PKK' and sent to the 'anti-terror unit' for interrogation.

We took three PKK guerrillas prisoner in the same engagement. The captain lined them up and ordered their summary execution. It was the same commander who had reproved the soldiers for cutting the ears off the dead. You have taken them prisoner, but who gives you the right to execute them? I was with a friend from Diyarbakir, tears were falling from his eyes. 'I want to kill this captain,' he said. On our way we saw two PKK guerrillas' corpses. Their heads were crushed with rocks by their comrades who did not want them to be identified. One of them must have been a woman for her hair was so long.

I only really became aware of my ethnic Kurdish origins during military service. Until then I believed all men were equal – I still believe that – but initially I didn't know about this PKK. I asked myself: 'What does being a Kurd mean?'

I used to believe in military service; it was a way of safeguarding the country. Against whom? Against the enemies of the people. It could be the PKK or Greece. Then I believed the slogan 'the PKK is evil'; now I have seen how oppressed the people of the East are. I regret I went for military service; now I would not go. My nephew was studying in the police academy. Just 20 days before his graduation he was expelled because he was a Kurd. Why should I serve the army? I feel terribly offended. I feel they simply use me.

Even those who most hate the PKK would not choose to do their
military service under these terrible conditions. The happy, healthy,
smiling soldiers in the TV ads are an illusion; the reality is the opposite,
it is terrible.

When they are surrounded the PKK do not aim at the soldiers, they
aim at officers. The officers rip off their badges to avoid death. But the
PKK still spots them: they don't carry bags, their boots are better quality,
the man next to them carries an extra load.

2 MARCH 1995

If I had known on which side of the road the mines were laid, I
wouldn't have sat on that side of the bus. There I was, sitting with my
gun beside me. It dashed through my mind: 'Fuck, there could be mines
here.' The weather is so hot. My eyes are closing. Just as I am about to
drop off comes the explosion. I'm thrown up, I fly towards the door, I
see the floor of the bus torn apart. OK? Suddenly the floor splits wide
open. I'm thrown out. A short moment of darkness, I'm out of it
Someone taps me on the back: 'Boy, your time's not up yet; we'll send
you back home.' Now I'm fully conscious, lying near the rear door.
There's no-one else in the bus; I'm crying. I try to sit up; I can't feel the
lower part of my body. I've lost my legs. I'm so calm I ask myself: 'Am I
stupid or am I brave?' Your life is ruined but still you wonder what's
happened to the others. Someone hugs you, says: 'OK. It's nothing.'
Officers come, they say: 'OK, boy. No problem.' Yet all the time you
know something's happened.

I had to stay four or five days in Sirnak. Then I was taken by a
helicopter to Diyarbakir. They couldn't do the surgery there so I was
taken on to GATA [military hospital in Ankara]. I had four operations. I
saw one of my legs was already amputated. I begged the doctor: 'Don't
cut! I can't go back to mum like this.' I thought of committing suicide in
hospital. But this was so easy, so cheap. The doctor said: 'We can't save
the other, we have to amputate.' Amputate then!

Without legs, others see you as belonging to an inferior physical
category. You are all alone.

And the dogs: don't underestimate the dogs. They never attack
soldiers and never step on the mines. Their strong sense of smell has

often saved a team from ambush. Nor would the mules step on mines. In the Yekmal post, a dog named *Katil* [Killer] went for a boy and tore him to pieces.

Being down there strengthens one's belief in God. We were going out on duty in snow two metres deep but neither our hands nor our feet were frozen. You start to think yes; there is a creator. But God takes sides in these clashes.

In the region I was in, there were hardly any impoverished villages. The smugglers, if they are on the army's side, are tolerated. Have you ever heard of trafficking in greens? They hire day labourers with mules from northern Iraq for 25 cents a day and smuggle eggplants and tomatoes on mule-back. The guy speaks no Turkish, yet every time he crosses the border he waves his hand and I respond.

Poverty is the root of everything. A man with a full stomach would not resort to arms.

The area was all mountains. But suddenly you would see orchards as surprising as an oasis in a desert. Short trees, cold springs.

Daily I see people losing their lives and others profitting from this. Some rob others. Most of the public are such assholes. If only they could see the realities of this war, just once. It's not just Kurds and Turks, all the citizens of this country are being robbed. They say the war costs US$80 billion. Imagine how many universities could have been built with that.

The Kurds say: 'The state does nothing for the Kurds.' You bastards! You've elected scores of deputies and ministers. Even presidents were elected from among the Kurds. Are not these the same people who prevent public investment in the Kurdish provinces?

Turkish nationalism, Kurdish nationalism – it's all the same. Instead of loving each other we are making war. We have been living side by side for thousands of years until there is no real difference left. After all I have seen, I am against the idea that this region is specifically Kurdish. Why? You can't distinguish a homogenous Kurdish race. I laugh at anyone who claims to be pure Kurd. People from the Mardin province are totally different from those in Diyarbakir. The region was invaded by Turks in 1071, almost 1,000 years ago. You can't deny history. Turkey is at the centre of the world.

It's hard to live here and equally hard to leave. Our country is really beautiful, I truly love it. Scores of ethnic groups live here. Some speak

Pontiac, some Kurdish, some Zaza. My mum, for instance, speaks Bulgarian.

It is very difficult to fight on the mountains. Nobody wants war, neither Turks, nor Kurds. Who benefits? It must be someone since Turkey is always importing weapons. A fighter plane cost US$30m; US$5m is spent on the war every day. It's not cheap to maintain 200,000 troops; in 1994 one G3 assault rifle bullet cost US$1. Hand grenades are imported from the US; rifle grenades are imported from Germany. War is money: it costs US$1,000 just to launch one helicopter. Why this war? It is meaningless. Most of the soldiers are not even aware of what's going on. Those on the mountains are devoted to their cause; but the conscripts are forced to leave their jobs to come to war. They die and then there is revenge and hate. This will accumulate and explode in the future, yielding more death and pain.

Previously I was a calm, quiet type. But now I could explode at the slightest provocation. This might be what they call the 'Vietnam Syndrome'. I can hardly control myself; I want to beat people up.

That's a joke of course, but sometimes I do feel I could shoot someone.

Have I killed anyone? I don't know. I don't think so. Maybe I have. I don't think about this much, but I don't think I could kill somebody now; everybody has the right to live Since we have not consciously fought for a cause it would be absurd to name us *gazi* [in Islam, a fighter who has survived a just war]. Victory is dusk. You have survived another night.

WE MUST LEARN TO LIVE TOGETHER

Before operations, most write letters and place them in their breast pocket. Scores of letters would pour out of their corpses when they were killed. They write things like: 'By the time my letter reaches you, I shall already be dead,' and so on.

On an ambush you've got to do silly things to overcome your fear; you sing, read magazines like *Playboy* or *Penthouse* until it's dark. I read the same issue at least 10 times. I didn't want to think; I didn't want to sleep. You could be killed in your sleep. Once, one of the guards ordered a conscript to stand in for him and went to sleep. The boy was listening to music on a Walkman, earphones plugged in. He couldn't hear the sound at his back; his throat was cut and those of the three others. When the sun rose no-one came down from the hill.

A friend of mine was killed. There was only one shot that night and it killed him. When we were on guard we used to smoke under a blanket so that the glow of the cigarette couldn't be seen. But he made a mistake. They saw the light; the bullet hit him in the mouth. Their snipers are really sharp.

Several wars are going on simultaneously down there. First and foremost, there's the fight against yourself. War is not fought only with weapons. You fight against yourself and, sometimes, your buddy.

We have interrogated POWs. Most are drug addicts. A local man owns a small plot of land and grows cannabis or opium. He doesn't use it himself but sells it. The PKK buys and processes. In our army, too, drug use is widespread, mostly crack.

We were close to the people. We used to go into town to shop; there was also a small billiard saloon where we played. The locals are really in search of their identity. They are serious and solemn people. They are illiterate but they speak out boldly. They have accepted Turkish citizenship. They don't claim a separate Kurdish state. They don't want it.

They have demands. That's normal. He's paying his taxes, he has a right to make his demands. The Kurds are not terrorists as some people would have it. His family has been ruined by the PKK; how could he be on their side. We need some institution to effect reconciliation; TV should air some serials; something.

I had Kurdish friends. They told me about their suffering. I'm not a Kurd. But there are Kurds, Armenians, Alevites and Sunnites in this country. We must learn to live together. The people of the region should not be blamed. They should have been educated. I had a very limited understanding of the question before going for military service. Turkey should invest here and give extensive education. They know nothing but honesty, but they are illiterate. Most of them cannot speak Turkish. If they are not educated this war will never end.

Corruption is widespread. A captain owns a modest car, but a non-commissioned officer might very well drive a BMW. This is absurd. And we die for that. Who dies for whom? There, the war is fought for money, to fill pockets.

I had finished my military service, I had missed everything. Three days after coming home I was out, sitting on a bank by the sea watching the sea and sipping my beer. Police officers came over asked to see my ID. One of them ordered me to stand up and put my hands up against a tree. I asked: 'What have I done, brother?' But one of them pointed his gun at me in reply. I put my hands on the tree but I am so nervous I can hardly stop myself crying: I have done this to others. Suddenly I twist and strike him with my elbow. I grab his gun.

He might have shot me for that. Fifty of them came over and laid in to me. I threw the gun away and started to cry. When they found out in the police station that I was a newly demobbed soldier they wanted to make up with me. I didn't apologise. I was ready to go to prison. They closed the file. I never used to resort to violence. I never even carried a pocketknife.

But after military service I carried a gun for a long time. I started frequenting bars, drank heavily and got violent. I couldn't stand injustice. I feel I should have controlled myself; I wasn't like that in the past.

I took two women from Istanbul's luxury district Bebek in my taxi; the radio was reporting casualties from the front. I said: 'What a pity, people are dying every day.' There was no response; they simply wanted to get home as soon as possible, perhaps to get ready to go out that night. The oldies are better; they care what happens there. I get angry at the insensitivity of people. ❏

Nadire Mater is a journalist. In addition to her work as a correspondent for Inter Press Services (IPS), she is the representative for Reporters Sans Frontières in Turkey

GEOFFREY ROBERTSON

Court in the act

In the wake of a war fought for 'ethical values', what price a permanent international criminal tribunal?

At the close of the 20th century, the dominant motive in world affairs is the quest – almost the thirst – for justice, replacing even the objective of regional security as the first principle of international action. That explains, at least at a jurisprudential level, the refusal to accept Chile's sovereign immunity for Pinochet or Serbian sovereignty over Kosovo, and the convoluted political arrangements made to put on trial the two Libyan intelligence officials suspected of planting the bomb which in 1988 took 259 lives above Lockerbie and 11 on the ground below. The tenacity of the Lockerbie relatives, although at first their cause seemed hopeless, drew in the UN and many world leaders, negotiating eventually – in April 1999 – a surrender of the Libyans for trial under Scottish law on an airbase in the Netherlands. In the same month, the Arusha Tribunal announced the capture in Cameroon of three former Rwandan government ministers suspected of planning the 1994 atrocities, including the foreign minister (who broadcast appeals to 'kill all Tutsis') and the ambassador who lied to the Security Council to cover up the genocide. Also in the same month, the UN finally sent a special envoy to Cambodia to demand the trial of Khmer Rouge leaders before an international tribunal. What these events presage is the end of sovereign impunity, a recognition that political leadership (a role for which there is no shortage of candidates in any country) carries as a concomitant of wielding State power an accountability for abusing it. Cynics might point out the present and pragmatic limitation of this principle, namely that it does not apply to high officials of states with a permanent seat on the Security Council. However, if the principle means there will be no more Rwandas, at least it will mean something. And then the challenge will be to invest the international legal system with the power – or failing that, the respect – to investigate the legitimacy of behaviour like China's in Tibet or Russia's in Chechnya or America's in firing missiles at a pharmaceutical factory in the Sudan. That challenge, as superpower opposition to the Rome Statute demonstrated, will take many years to prevail, but the best start is to get the International Criminal Court up and running as early as possible. Justice, once there is a procedure for its delivery, is prone to have its own momentum.

In the 21st century the human rights movement will struggle on against its traditional enemies – armies, Churches and states – looking increasingly to international law to provide a lever against these institutional powers. The Pentagon organised a global campaign to undermine the International Criminal Court, ensuring that commanders in most of its client countries lobbied governments against the idea. (What was hopeful and heartening was that it failed – in every country except the USA.) Transnational religion has proved a forceful opposition to women's rights, especially after the collapse of communism. In Afghanistan under Russian puppet governance, women made up half the doctors and university students and most of the teachers, but the Taliban fundamentalists refuse to allow women to work or to study, or even to venture outside the home without a male relative. The problem is not only with Islam: a resurgence of Roman Catholicism in eastern Europe has been particularly damaging to women's rights – Lech Walesa lost his civil liberties halo when as president of Poland he vetoed abortion reform, and the Vatican aroused widespread disgust by trying to stop supplies of 'morning-after' pills reaching refugee women raped by Serb battalions during the cleansing of Kosovo. Vatican diplomacy has blessed most of the tyrants and torturers of recent history, betraying Catholic idealists in Singapore to Lee Kuan Yew and secretly exerting pressure on the British government to free the unpenitent General Pinochet.

As for governments, realpolitik still rules when human rights come up against superpower interests. China remains deeply suspicious of any international legal development which threatens sovereignty. It persists in treating advocacy of democracy as a crime punishable with upwards of 10 years in prison, but since it boasts the world's largest army – 2.5 million soldiers – and possesses nuclear bombs and intercontinental ballistic missiles, no-one is prepared to argue with it very strenuously. France blows hot and cold on human rights: it is not above committing terrorist crimes (the sinking of the *Rainbow Warrior*) and its record in francophone Africa includes arming genocidal Hutu and harbouring President Mobutu, for long the world's most corrupt ruler. In December 1998, France hosted the fiftieth birthday celebrations for the Universal Declaration at the Palais Chaillot in Paris; it refused to invite Chinese democrats or Tibetan representatives, for fear of upsetting Beijing.

Then, of course, there is the problem of the United States, a nation much given to spurts of world leadership followed by periods of self-regarding isolationism. Its scholars have made vast contributions to the literature of human rights, reflecting its history as the land of the free, but its refusal to qualify its own sovereignty in any way by accepting international jurisdiction reduces its influence and sets bad examples. As the only true superpower, the US will determine the 'humanitarian necessity' for any intervention without UN approval, but haphazardly (ignoring genocide in Rwanda but not in Serbia) and without clear or objective criteria. It has become 'bomb happy', in the sense that the Mogadishu factor can only be circumvented by high-flying aerial attacks that risk no American lives, but imperil many innocent civilians below – a tactic of questionable morality. Unless it shows greater consistency in its approach to human rights (it has been notably protective of 'friends' such as Israel and Saudi Arabia) and some eventual willingness to bind itself to the justice it prescribes for others, its emergence as the 'benign hegemon' (in Samuel Huntingdon's phrase) will make for partisan and inequitable human rights enforcement.

Unfortunately, in the US, human rights do not begin at home, and certainly not in jail: conditions in some state penitentiaries are barbaric, as women prisoners are routinely assaulted and both male and female convicts are made (particularly in the south) to serve on chain gangs, and 'hog-tied' with their wrists bound to their ankles, and kept in line by guards who use chemical sprays and electric prods. The provisions for legal representation of the poor are uniformly inadequate in this richest of nations, and death penalties are applied with scant regard to ECOSOC [Economic and Social Council] standards. The US is a country which plans to 'disappear' almost as many of its citizens as did Pinochet, namely the 3,500 currently condemned to die on its death rows. Somalia stands alongside the US as the only country that refuses to ratify the Convention on the Rights of the Child (because it wants to execute juveniles and to recruit teenage soldiers) and its bedfellows in objecting to the ICC were China, Libya, Iraq, Algeria, Sudan and Iran. In 1999 the team of pliant law professors it had sent to Rome to sabotage the ICC statute were redeployed to collect evidence of Serbian war crimes in Kosovo: the nation that refuses to be bound by international human rights law now demands the prosecution of foreigners who violate it. As the one great superpower with pretensions to police the world, its opposition to the ICC and the Landmines Convention show it up as a truculent and tragic opponent of the demand for *universal* human rights.

The most significant change in the human rights movement as it goes into the millennium is that it will go on the offensive. The past has been a matter of pleading with tyrants, writing letters and sending missions to beg them not to act cruelly. That will not be necessary if there is a possibility that they can be deterred, by threats of humanitarian or UN intervention or with nemesis in the form of the International Criminal Court. Human rights discourse will in future be less pious and less 'politically correct'. We will become a little more sophisticated about humanitarian aid (remembering how the British government used this as an excuse when supplying AIDS-testing kits to the Iraqi army, never bothering to find out what happened to a soldier who tested positive). Although the 21st century will have its share of despots, they will be fewer and in the absence of the Cold War they will not have a super-power support. There will no longer be any need to say, as FDR said of Grandfather Somoza: 'He may be a son of a bitch, but he's our son of a bitch.'

But optimism about the future must be tempered by the dreadful failures of the past, and especially the failure of the UN, with its bureaucratic and politicised machinery, to implement the promises of the Universal Declaration in its first half-century (excluding refugees, it still spends less than 2% of its budget on human rights). Any post-mortem on NATO's bombing of Serbia must recognise the stark fact that in 1999 the Security Council was incapable of intervening to stop crimes against humanity in Kosovo because Russia chose to turn a blind eye and China's leaders could not care less about man's inhumanity to man. NATO stepped into the breach, overlooking the Srebrenica lesson that human rights offensives must have clearly stated objectives, of sufficient moral force to justify any casualties that may be necessary to achieve them. Cowardice in this cause is simply not an option, yet states prepared to kill were not prepared to sacrifice: the US insisted on high-altitude bombing that imperilled civilians while Italy and Germany refused to contemplate ground troops. This is an uneasy and unpopular beginning for the 'third age' of human rights enforcement, although it is likely to be remembered not for its military and political misjudgments, but as the first war waged for ethical principle alone, because, as Václav Havel put it: 'no decent person can stand by and watch the systematic state-directed murder of other people.' The commission of crimes against humanity provides an indisputable warrant for punishment of violator states. At the fag end of a century in which 160 million human lives have been wasted by war and genocide and torture, the world best remembers those its pledges have failed by determining that in the future, at whatever cost, it is going to make them stick. ❏

Geoffrey Robertson *has appeared as counsel in many human rights cases. He is also Visiting Professor in Human Rights at Birkbeck College. This extract is taken from* Crimes Against Humanity *(Penguin, 1999)*

PETER MORGAN

Sale of the decade

Despots eventually die, but their treasures outlive them and may raise a little cash for the countries they have bankrupted

In the last reel of *Citizen Kane*, Orson Welles produces a wonderful image of his tycoon's infinite wealth. After Kane's death, the Great Hall of Xanadu is filled with tapestries and statues, paintings and bric-a-brac; bulging crates and packing cases cram into the distance. Aside from the arty-smarty dialogue ('23 thousand bucks? That's a lot of money to pay for a dame without a head') the scene lingers mainly because it's been so widely imitated. From *Raiders of the Lost Ark* to *The X-Files,* we have learned to associate underground troves with despotism and sinister privilege.

Several months ago, Xanadu fact and fiction merged in an intriguing proposal. A Romanian journalist called Cristian Rautu rang Channel 4 News with a story that sounded too good to be true, too fantastic to be factual. Would we like to film Nicolae Ceaucescu's private fortune, he wondered, before it was auctioned off? At first, I didn't believe him. The whole thing felt too much like an Elmore Leonard caper: you knew that somehow, somewhere (Miami airport, probably), the story would fall apart. But then Cristian filled me in on the detail. Ceaucescu's private possessions had been stowed away after the 'Revolution' to stop a cult fermenting around the late, unlamented *Conducator*. Ten years on, Romania's debt-ridden ministry-of-state protocol had decided to put some of its vast collection of totalitarian tat up for sale. And so it came to pass that the Revolution was televised, and then sold off in small lots. What would we be able to film, I asked. 'Oh, cars, boats, fur coats … his nuclear bunker' came the reply. Two days later, I was in Bucharest.

Our first stop was a vast granite tower in the centre of the city. Under Ceaucescu, the communist mausoleum had been a forbidden, sacred site. The tombs surrounding the black obelisk in an obedient semi-circle

Party HQ – Credit: Leonard Freed/Magnum

contained the bodies of communist bosses. These days, stray dogs cock their legs on moss and weed, and teenage skateboarders run round the cracked paths. There's no decent word in English to describe the emotions (part fear and part mould) summoned by such places. Revulsion is one, I guess. In muted retirement, I found it hard to imagine the power and reverence that once coursed through these drab blocks: the relics of a forgotten religion. As if to reinforce this notion, the caretaker produced an episcopal brass key and twiddled with the lock. Behind the 10-foot-high door was the body of Gheorghe Gheorghiu-Dej, the founding leader of Communist Romania, interred here in the 1960s. After 1989, the mausoleum was also turned into the Ceaucescu's bargain basement: thousands of family knick-knacks were stashed inside because there was nowhere else for them to go.

At this point, I should make a somewhat embarrassing admission. There are moments when journalism demands a level head and mature judgment: an adult *hateur*, if you like. But there are also times when the job generates helpless excitement, and one behaves like a 10-year-old in a Nike shop. Sadly, this was one of those. For the first few minutes, all I can remember thinking (and saying) was: 'Wow, Oh my God, Look at that, Christ Almighty, Eurgh,' and various words to that effect. Cristian, too, was wandering round with a huge grin on his face. Analysis was overtaken by sheer, head-spinning amazement. The huge circular room was packed from floor to ceiling with every conceivable kind of gift and cast-off: hundreds of oil paintings of Nicolae and Elena (their countrymen reduced to an impressionist background blur); chalk-white busts of the First Couple; tables and chairs with 'NC' carved into the woodwork; magic carpets with Nicolae's block head woven into the thick cloth. If you wanted any reminder of the grotesque personality cult, bronze busts stood guard. Someone had dunked white paint into Nicolae and Elena's eyes, giving them an even more demonic cast than usual. I sunk two fingers into Nicolae's vacant sockets, and felt much the better for it.

Most of the objects stored inside the mausoleum were gifts from local party bosses. A scale model of a hydroelectric project; a wooden shield from the cheery teenagers of Timisoara; a silver pit-head donated by 'The Grateful Miners of the Jiu Valley'. Each item had been tagged and dated: this was the kind of faithless, mediocre stuff politicians get given every day of the year. Wandering round this collection, I wondered whether Elizabeth Windsor has a similar store under Buckingham Palace. Where else would she put all those cross-eyed dolls and obscene wood carvings that seem to accumulate on royal tours? Of course, it's easy to be facetious. Faced with such a barrage of tack, you forget the climate in which many of these objects were presented. You forget the fear: the trembling hand of a local *apparat* as he offers his gift; the leader's cretinous glare.

There was, however, a certain satisfaction in seeing the remains of one regime being piled on top of another. Before we left the freezing vault, Cristian had one more query. He had heard (in the mysterious way that folk myths swirl around a city) that there was an embalming room beneath Gheorghiu-Dej's tomb. The caretaker shrugged. It was a secret, but what was the point of secrets any more. Using the camera light as our guide, we went down another flight of stairs and into a white-walled corridor. Here was the sanctum within the sanctum: a small, antiseptic operating theatre with a grey, rectangular slab at its centre. The bodies of communist worthies were brought here for posthumous cosmetic surgery; no doubt Nicolae and Elena would have joined them by now if their journeys had not been so rudely interrupted. Six months later, I can still summon the immense silence of that room, and can relive the slight nausea induced by the mortuary slab and the steel washbowl placed, businesslike, in one corner.

What remains too is the banality of these places. After the initial rush of schoolboy excitement, I started to look at Nicolae's possessions with a more critical eye. And frankly, his taste was pretty erratic. This was confirmed the next day when we drove out to Lake Snagov, to the north of Bucharest. Ceaucescu built a Californian-style villa here in the mid-1980s, one of the last retreats from the dystopic world he had created. The 'palace' was a long, low complex with phony Italianate gardens. The most striking – and rather sad – feature of the Ceaucescu's weekend retreat was the way it strained to feel foreign. There was a sun terrace and indoor pool, a gymnasium (with medicine balls) and private cinema: everything was designed to make the First Couple feel they were elsewhere in the world, anywhere but in their beloved Romania. At least that was one thing the Ceaucescus had in common with their subjects.

There were also despotic details that would not have looked out of place in a Hollywood film, and we found it hard not to laugh. A map of the world, painted fresco style on a study wall with Romania highlighted at its centre; an electric sun roof above the swimming pool; a pair of yellow silk chairs for the Ceaucescus' dogs to lap up the sun. We were shown around by the couple's former housekeeper. What were Nicolae and Elena like, we wondered. 'Very correct, very proper,' she said. 'We kept the house ready for them at all times. When they arrived, we were not allowed to have eye contact with them.' The housekeeper implied this was because the Ceaucescus were naturally modest and retiring. It also sounded like a sound policy against assassination. Before leaving, the elderly lady showed us the bedroom where Michael Jackson had stayed in 1994, when he performed in Bucharest. An old colour TV set stood at one end of the room, a bed at the other. They were about 30 feet apart. Despots die, presidents are overthrown. But powerful people still need buildings to give themselves shape and definition.

When Romanians talk of the Ceaucescus as 'our most marketable monsters since Dracula', there's a catch in their voices. No-one wants to dwell on the past; the anger directed at those lost, missing years still surfaces in conversation, particularly with young people ('We only had two hours of television a day! We missed so much good music!'). But money has to be made, IMF loans to be paid. If 1989 showed that people across Europe could reclaim their history, then 1999 has seen that history turned into packaged spectacle. The Snagov Palace is now open for bed and breakfast; Ceaucescu's grotesque House of the Republic offers guided tours and conference facilities. Fewer visitors make it to the cemeteries that contain the victims of Ceaucescu's rule.

Cristian had one last surprise. While rooting around the cellars of Snagov Palace, he had found some old feature films stored in calf-bound cases. These were hour-long tributes to the great leader, filmed during the annual *Omagiu* in Bucharest. Thousands of schoolchildren and factory workers were drilled in a performance of flag-waving-and-banner-bearing, modelled on the vast ego trips Ceaucescu had seen for Kim II Sung in North Korea. We viewed several hours of this material, watching the same dutiful faces march past the camera, waving to the Great Leader and his wife. 'If you want to know what life was really like at that time,' said Cristian, 'just look at those people's faces. No-one is smiling.' ❏

Peter Morgan is a reporter with Channel 4 News, UK

Support for

Index on Censorship and the *Writers and Scholars Educational Trust (WSET)* were founded to protect and promote freedom of expression. The work of maintaining and extending freedoms never stops. Freedom of expression is not self-perpetuating but has to be maintained by constant vigilance.

The work of *Index* and *WSET* is only made possible thanks to the generosity and support of our many friends and subscribers worldwide. We depend on donations to guarantee our independence; to fund research and to support projects which promote free expression.

The Trustees and Directors would like to thank the many individuals and organisations who support *Index on Censorship* and *Writers and Scholars Educational Trust*, including:

If you would like more information about *Index on Censorship* or would like to support our work, please contact Hugo Grieve, Fundraising Manager, on (44) 171 278 2313 or e-mail hugo@indexoncensorship.org

In *Word Power*, the 2/99 issue of *Index*, we referred to a database on freedom of expression in the twentieth century which is being handed over to the new Alexandria Library. *Index* wishes to make it clear that it is only one of a large number of international organisations which are partners in this project. More importantly, the Norwegian Forum for Freedom of Expression is the sole originator of this project, which has been entirely funded by the Norwegian Ministry of Culture, as Norway's gift to the new library. The Minister of Culture will deliver the database to the Alexandria Library when it opens in 2000.

MARK THOMPSON

Communicating fear

The role of the media in forging war in former Yugoslavia was more complex than is often argued

Leaving aside the question whether the war in Yugoslavia could have been started without systematic media manipulation, this manipulation was certainly intrinsic to the strategies of various leaders. The most influential media were used to obtain public support or mere tolerance for policies which, at best, were bound to threaten the peace, security and prosperity of all peoples in the region and, at worst, were sheer belligerence. This support or tolerance could not have been assured unless the public accepted that armed conflict would not be an excessive price for the pursuit of nationalist objectives, invariably presented as the defence of national kin and culture.

The media were essential to procure such acceptance. They were and are indispensable conduits for disinformation, propaganda, half-truths and so forth. They promoted certain information and opinions while suppressing or marginalising others. The result? As the Report of the International Commission on the Balkans, *Unfinished Peace* said: 'The public is not able to inform itself about the actions of government. Lacking elementary information about the motives and intentions of its leaders, it has been kept blindfolded and disoriented'. As for the effect of ethnic propaganda on public perceptions, it can be measured. Research in 1997 by S Malesevic and G Uzelac into the 'perception of other ethnic groups' among students at Zagreb University in May 1992 and June 1993 has indicated the power of the media to influence these attitudes. In May 1992, when the first sample was taken, 'the distance towards the Muslims was the lowest in comparison with that expressed

towards other ex-Yugoslav ethnic groups'. The second sample showed a
dramatic change: now the Muslims 'were classified in the same manner
and in the same category as Serbs and Montenegrins'. The researchers
noted that the change 'would not be so striking if the respondents had
actually experienced Muslim misdeeds or atrocities personally. In this
case, when the entire war was perceived through the media, it can be
concluded that the same media, at least partially, induced an increase in
the social distance.' Between May 1992 and June 1993: 'Croats from
Croatia read in their daily newspapers about their new enemy – the
Muslims.' (They also, of course, watched and heard the same message on
their television sets and radios.) In sum, the media 'thus served as an
instrument for the legitimisation of the actions of the Croatian political
elite'.

Yet the analysis of the role of media should not end with a critique of
media messages – as if nothing need be said about how the messages
achieve their effect, how they operate. Media also served authority by
virtue of their status as political institutions in society. Public
preconceptions of mass media were formed in these countries during
long experience of authoritarian government.

The continuity of authoritarianism up to the present day, despite (or
partly because of) the violent destruction of the Titoist system, finds
illumination in a profound metaphorical analogy drawn by Polish
journalist Konstanty Gebert, remarking on the post-communist
transition in Europe. '[W]hen you translate from the language of
communism into the language of democracy, you need to change both
the *vocabulary* and the *grammar*,' Gebert says. 'It is a very difficult and
complicated task. However, if you want to translate from the language of
communism into the language of nationalism, all you need to change is
the vocabulary. The grammar remains the same. The type of mental
structures that the new system builds up are based on the foundations
that already existed under communism. It is us versus them, it is
inclusion versus exclusion, and violence as a legitimate way of achieving
previously ideological, and now national, goals.'

A popular fear of politics, usually expressed as disgust, is a sensible
reaction to the use by authority of the politics of fear. Inheriting this
resource intact, along with the institutional means (the mass media) to
produce it, the post-communist regimes have understood this very well.
Using the media to help preserve a totally ideological conception of

politics, they propose themselves as champions of the national interest, above mere sordid 'politics'. This in turn explains why the regimes often behave, especially under pressure, as if independent media pose a greater threat to them than opposition parties. Especially in Serbia, these media have repeatedly proven to be less corruptible than the opposition politicians; hence they can lay a more convincing claim to the uncontaminated moral heights, witnessing against fear and against the obedience that fear breeds.

The continuity of authoritarianism in these countries includes a continuity of attitudes to mass media by government but also by the public. Studies show that a majority of people distrust pro-regime media while continuing to consume them, and often share the general political perspective of these media regardless of the fact that this perspective reflects the same bias that renders the media untrustworthy in the first place. Most glaring in the case of Serbia, this paradox is also obvious in Croatia. We may assume that data from Bosnia would point in the same forked directions.

There are, to be sure, some mundane reasons why people remain loyal consumers of media they don't trust. Dusan Reljic of *Vreme* magazine observed that 'gaining access to alternative information is costly and time-consuming. Moreover, only a few people dare to confront their political environment, their neighbours, their families by signalling disbelief or even dissent with government opinion.' Reljic has suggested elsewhere that the 'clash between the rational perception that public television and other media in the lap of the authorities consciously misinform, and the decision not to stop consuming information identified as false, is obviously suppressed in the individual consciousness. The conclusion implies that the need to remain part of the homogenised mass is stronger than the realisation that this is false information which may lead to wrong decisions.'

Yet *is* it so obvious that people 'suppress' the 'clash'? Or does this collision rather belong to the manifest burden of everyday stress, of cognitive dissonance, borne by citizens in these societies? As for 'wrong decisions', wrong for whom? Anthropologist Ivan Colovic has observed that media are widely regarded as notice-boards or traffic lights, suggesting experience has shaped expectations and behaviour. In other words, if people usually sense or understand that the pro-regime media are actually designed to communicate veiled directives, why would they treat these media as if they were anything else? Especially if the same authorities who 'talk through the newspapers' also wield vast influence in career and commercial patronage, employment, housing and education?

Media credibility and public credulity in a society cannot be assessed in isolation from the role of power. Except in totalitarian states, media are Janus-faced structures, straddling the frontier between State and civil society, looking both ways and feeding from both sources (not in equal measure). Censorship and propaganda are notoriously unreliable tools, prone to spotlight what they seek to conceal, subverting their own objectives with unintended irony. Media cannot rid words and images of their ambiguities, their recesses of meaning. Editors are subject to error and influence. Political weather changes in accordance with climatic patterns that lie beyond the control of particular regimes. When media resist these changes, the denial is itself a give-away. For these reasons too, media can retain a loyalty, even credibility, among people who do not trust them.

The appeal of television seems to draw a good deal upon fear, including the thrill and pang of public fears funnelled ethereally into private homes. Fear engenders hatred and also fosters dependence on authority figures, the cult of whose personalities is celebrated and policed by the same media that disseminate the fear. 'Ethnic hatred' has mistakenly (often self-servingly) been accepted by the outside world as the cause of war: an expression of deeply ingrained animosity. This hatred was, however, implanted and cultivated. 'What we witnessed was violence-provoking nationalism from the top down,' recalls Warren Zimmermann, 'inculcated primarily through the medium of television. Any ætiology of the war which underrates this factor has condemned itself to superficiality, whether journalistic or professorial.

Overall, the discourse about the wars in the former Yugoslavia suggests that the lesson of thinkers from Nietzsche to Barthes, that *myth* converts *history* into *nature*, still counts for little outside universities. Few commentators tried to expose the wisdom about ingrained animosities for what it is: a political myth based on a highly selective reading of recent history, peddled by Serb and Croat nationalists (who argue that the peoples in conflict are divided by civilisational differences equivalent to those between races, if not species), but also taken up by western politicians wanting alibis for their neutralism or timidity in Bosnia (*Index*

3&4/99).

The emotions promoted in the first place by the Serbian media could not have bewitched society without the resort to massive violence which, by provoking counter-attacks, seemed to authenticate the prior propaganda. Yet this violence launched by Serbia and its proxies against Croatia and Bosnia, where it was inevitably reciprocated, was no 'natural' expression, regardless of how adroitly the instigators of violence exploited certain existing inter-ethnic animus. As for Serbian and Croatian strategies in Bosnia, they fomented fear, hatred and racism with two objectives: to homogenise people into national or ethnic constituencies, and thereby capture wide support; and to displace the responsibility for these strategies back on to those same constituencies. The latter motive was especially strong in Serbia, for a simple reason: Milosevic was determined to preserve deniability regarding his sponsorship of rebellion and aggression. Deniability would have been impossible to sustain if influential mass media had been free to investigate the conspiracies.

Milosevic's skill in displacing responsibility can be gauged by the way that, during the decisive early phase of the war, the outside world had the impression that it really was the people driving Milosevic and not vice versa. The other regimes soon pulled the same stunt. Observing the war from nearby Trieste, Claudio Magris noted 'the ability of the leaders to create artificially, in the laboratory, a presumptive *vox populi*'.

It becomes clear why explicit control over influential media was the regime's goal, especially at volatile moments such as the Milosevic-Holbrooke negotiations over Kosovo. Media being what they are, such control served a twofold function. Controlled media supplied a highly visible and influential model of daily obedience to the party-state. Watching the evening news on television, the public consumed the party-state's propaganda and, by paying respect to party-state power, confirmed that power. Second, these media demonstrated the regime's will to dominate the range of independent or intermediate ('public service') institutions which in a real democracy would be the pillars of civil society. By the same token the absence or loss of such control tended to demonstrate the reverse: that the regime lacked the nerve or resolve to impose itself upon society, which – it would follow – might be able and even entitled to free itself from that imposition.

Mass media serving as tools for civic and social disempowerment: it is a grim prospect, remote from visions beheld in earlier decades by media theorists celebrating the democratic accessibility of electronic media, their promise of ever more interactivity, reversing the industrial trend that for the past century and a half had concentrated production in ever fewer hands while dispersing consumption ever more widely. Three decades or so ago, it could seem that revolutions in media technology would entail democratic breakthroughs on the political front.

In the former Yugoslavia, above all in Serbia, this dialectic has cut the other way – as if the darkest premonitions of the New Left, about the imposition of social discipline by capitalist media, had been confirmed in the domain of Europe's last communist ruler. The monologue has rejuvenated itself and trampled down the shoots of interactivity. This time, the monologue's name is *ethnocentricity*.

Serbs were the most intensively targeted, that is to say ethnically constructed, audience in crisis-torn Yugoslavia. Was it by coincidence that they were also the most *inert* group, the collective most willing to invest its entire trust in authority figures and to keep on investing, however catastrophic the returns? For the media manipulation was rarely designed to rouse the masses to act. Analysing the Belgrade press in the late 1980s, when the Milosevic regime staged a series of mass rallies in Serbia and Montenegro, the sociologist Svetlana Slapsak concluded that 'the rallies are not decisive for mobilising the masses but rather, above all, for manipulating and controlling the public which was presumed not to take part in the rallies'. Mere negative assent was the response sought by the media, for recycling by those same media as proof of overwhelming support.

The same holds for Croatia's somewhat less successful strategy in Bosnia and Herzegovina. Obedience has been more devastating in the latter-day Balkans than any fabled wildness or savagery, and this obedience seems indistinguishable from the 'behavioural inertia' that typifies the consumer of electronic media, for whom interactivity – including the pseudo interactivity of television – does not assist but rather replaces 'traditional mobilising activity'.

When Rupert Murdoch said a few years ago that technology had abolished the tyranny of distance, it was a salesman's boast rather than a scientist's eureka, one often heard since the invention of the telegraph. But anyone who discussed the Croatian or Bosnian wars with the citizens of, say, Belgrade while those wars were going on knows that technology can help *create* distance. Television can be used to calibrate and entrench the gap between an audience and an event. By the early 1990s, when right-wing populists in the USA were giving those old dreams of interactivity their only foreseeable fulfilment by preaching the possibilities of 'virtual democracy', Europe's war was making it difficult not to notice that television is a pseudo-interactive medium, or even *anti*-interactive, with a bag of tricks for disguising monologue as dialogue.

Does not the literal passivity of television-watchers, defined by their posture of acquiescence, serve to confirm an explicit message that viewers should trust their leaders?

Be this as it may, events in Serbia, Croatia and Bosnia during the 1990s showed that popular access to information markets can still be drastically curtailed by governments in Europe. These events have also proven that the authority of 'national information' is highly resilient. Far from dragging political change in its wake, media technology has been harnessed to traditional values and to anachronistic, indeed barbarous agendas. Far from undermining the producers' monopoly and abolishing the dominion of literacy, the media here provided belligerent regimes with a precious means to enhance their power. Neo-tribal messages transmit very nicely by microwave link.

As for *why* television is highly convenient to regimes that depend upon authoritarian neo-tribalism, Benedict Anderson's theory of nations as 'imagined communities' remains suggestive. The theory allots cultural activity a central part in fabricating the sense of nationality. And culture was the ground on which nations were recently homogenised and political strategies justified in the former Yugoslav republics. Political conflicts were waged in the names of culture. Particulars of language, custom, folklore and confession, mythologised versions of history, the full rigmarole of 'ethnicity' were enthroned as the supreme principles of individual existence and collective (political) destiny – the narcissism of minor difference magnified to despotic proportions. With their 'incomparable power of suggestion', electronic media were a superb resource for defining the values and agendas that feed the imaginary of imagined communities.

Without the siege-mentality of wartime, deprivations and abuses become less tolerable. Perhaps a post-war mood crystallised in November 1996, a tidy year after Dayton, with the public protests in Belgrade and

Zagreb. Raymond Williams's affirmation, addressed to a very different context, is valid here: 'Too few people are speaking to and for too many in conditions in which, increasingly, they nevertheless cannot prevent others from acting and failing to act.' In short, the regime's space for manoeuvre has diminished and will diminish further. ❏

Mark Thompson wrote A Paper House: the Ending of Yugoslavia *(Vintage, 1992). The revised edition of his* Forging War: The Media in Serbia, Croatia, Bosnia and Herzegovina *is published by ARTICLE 19 in association with University of Luton Press. To order your copy contact: Book Representation and Distribution Ltd, Tel: +44 (0) 1702 552 912 Fax: +44 (0) 1702 556 095 e.mail brpd@netcomuk.co.uk This excerpt © ARTICLE 19*

INDEX TALKS

'The wall that straddled Berlin for 28 years was a powerful symbol of a city divided against itself. And more: it stood for the separation of people and ideologies worldwide. When it fell on 10 November 1989, it did not drag down those walls that continue to separate nations and cities.' – Judith Vidal-Hall

Index, and contributors to this issue, will mark the 10th Anniversary of the fall of the Berlin Wall with a discussion on what will shape international relations in the next century. Join us for:

After the fall; the walls remain

**THE ICA, THE MALL
LONDON SW1**

**10 NOVEMBER 1999
at 7.30pm**

**Tickets: £6, £5 (concs.), £4 (Index subscribers &
ICA members) – call ICA box office: 0171 930 3647
Panel details – call Index Marketing Dept: 0171 278-2313**

'The banner held aloft in the belief that men are united by a common humanity has been torn down and one announcing that we are what we consume has been raised in its place.'
– Santiago Kovadloff

Institute of Contemporary Arts

YANG LIAN

Those who cannot return have come home

I've almost forgotten what it feels like to be a poet in his own country, but here I am. China is no longer a dream, but an unmistakable emotion. This ground is Chinese ground. But it is no longer my country: as the holder of a New Zealand passport, living in London and writing in the Chinese language, it is my very own foreign country.

Ten years ago, shortly before my expulsion, I wrote: 'All those non-persons who cannot return have come home.' Gradually, the focus of my memories narrows on to a small room. At its entrance hangs a sign in Chinese calligraphy, 'The hall of ghosts'; colourful traditional masks on the wall ward off evil; books stream from shelves on to a bed and table – the table is part school blackboard sawn in half; a bunch of crimson Chinese reeds I picked from among the ruins of the Perfect Bright Garden on the day my mother died surrounds her photograph; an urn, covered in a black cloth, holds my gaze as, in those last moments, the door slowly closes to me. Home is more real in my dreams. But do I recognise this China before my eyes?

The old city of Beijing has disappeared without trace. The chilly reflection of glass and steel swallowed small alleyways and the warmth of secluded courtyards. As a child, I craned my neck until it hurt to look up at the pagodas of Tianning Temple. Now they barely reach halfway up modern apartment blocks. The skyline, once dominated by tumultuous palace roofs, is brimming with Xitong-caps, as the city's taxi drivers call them: huge roofs in the traditional style, like reproduction antiques, simplified to a grotesque ugliness. And so popular with ex-mayor Chen Xitong that each new building's design had to have one if it were to pass his planning committee. Chen Xitong was forced out of power in 1997, but these monstrous appendages will defile this patch of sky for a 100 years.

During the Cultural Revolution, I was stationed in a unit in a far-off suburb. A clay road along which I once carried coffins is buried under the concrete foundations of a 3-star hotel; once a whole village would crowd around a TV, now every household owns a video recorder. Hoteliers wave their mobile phones; any intellectual worth his salt has an e-mail address; Internet access is the least any student expects by way of intellectual stimulation; and Mao's old idea that 'poverty is beautiful' has been completely superseded by the dictatorship of money. *Xiang qian lan* (Look ahead, but literally, Look toward money) is the order of the day. The old values are gone forever, but this is no guarantee that economic success will eventually lead to democracy and a new ethical code.

The possibility of attaining wealth ratchets up greed and breeds motivation. 'Investment' and 'shares' have replaced degenerate expressions from the 1980s like 'individual' and 'the self'. The meaning of 'choice' is horribly apparent to an unemployed labourer who has to live on just 200 yuan a month. The old city has disappeared and with it the ease of long ago. Walking around the glittering hoardings that advertise everything from Coca-Cola to cures for sexually transmitted diseases, I sense the sweet smell of wealth, and the stench of blood spilled in free-market competition.

Should I applaud, or weep? Applaud China for being more western than the West, and in such a short time? Weep because this bears no resemblance to the West I know? A song has been circulating in Shanghai since the Audi, manufactured in China now, became the official car of party cadres: 'Along a road four circles [Audi logo] glide/Open the door and look inside/Corrupt old sods! Shoot them quickly./Courts never find these bastards guilty.'

The government has issued countless decrees outlawing relations between the state and the private sector and has vehemently denounced corruption. Words are one thing, but it is something else altogether when your son is managing director of a certain firm,and your shares in that company, like your bank balance, continue to grow. As everyone knows, Mayor Chen Xitong was not fired for misappropriating several billion *yuan* of public funds. He lost the job he had secured in the wake of the 1989 massacre for his pretensions to power and, more important, for challenging Jiang Zemin.

But what of other corrupt officials who know the game well, swim with the tide and ingratiate themselves with the ruling 'Son of Heaven'? The Communist Party makes noises about its idealism, but cannot conceal its true nature, its naked desire for power and wealth. Yet for many Chinese, the 'Money Cultural Revolution' is not madness but something they can all share, official lies as well as the hallucinatory bravery of those who dissent form a single 'historical truth'. Where is 'history'? Where does 'the truth' come from, if not from financial returns? Chinese political apathy and the experience of successful money spinning complement each other. Lying on the floor of an old friend's apartment, drinking and talking late into the night, I found I had to agree: nothing can be worse than to be flung from dearth into abundance; nothing more shocking than to have been poor yesterday and today to command vast wealth!

Culture in China today is the so-called market economy with ideological regulations. A famous young writer quibbled with a TV station. He should have been paid 30,000 *yuan* (cUS$4,000) for a play he was able to write 'in two days, with the necessary alcohol'. 'Who picks the theme?' 'The station.' The play is called *The Chinese Girl* – a shameless piece of propaganda – and the money the necessary price for the writer's name. It's OK to make money and you can make it any way you chose. For instance, chequebook journalism is commonplace: no-one believes what they read in the paper. Even in supposedly more reputable academic and literary circles, everyone knows that the longer the panegyric at a book launch, the bigger the cheque.

Seeing intellectuals throw away their last scrap of conscience is as bad as hearing empty moral sermons, but no coincidence. At the beginning of the 1990s, 'loutish literature' was all the rage. With Wang Shou as its spokesman and 'nothing is serious' as its motto, it ousted literature that reflected serious social and cultural concerns. Shortly afterwards, Wang Shou was himself toppled by the next generation of new writers, and for exactly the same reasons: despite all his clowning around, he was 'too serious'. What does 'not serious' mean? One publishing group, recognising a strong nationalist tendency after the failure of China's bid to host the Olympic Games in 2000, caused a sensation both at home and abroad with a hastily written book, *China can say no* (Index 1/1997). But before they knew it – after Jiang Zemin's trip to the United States and Bill Clinton's to Beijing – China was involved in a huge power game over international trade agreements. So they quickly pushed out another, *China can't only say no*! If politics lose their principles, anyone can play with them. Indeed, today's artists, such as the exponents of Mao-Pop – propaganda images from the Cultural Revolution vulgarly glossed with Coca-Cola-style ads – successfully seek a wide audience. Western 'cultural tourists', along with party cadres with generous pay packets, are happy to buy goods with the brand name 'Chinese Art'. When everything has a price tag, the first thing to go is integrity.

Who is worst off in the new, official culture? Ultimately, Chinese culture itself. Superficial content and mediocre forms are the chief characteristics of artistic creation in mainland China. The difference between official and underground culture has been replaced by the contrast between 'commercial success' and 'poor but worthy' art. Why write? Write for whom? Who'll publish it? Who'll read it? Essentially, it's all a matter of taste.

In literature, for example, the use of the Cultural Revolution as a theme of stories and novels has turned into something of a nightmare. Twenty years on, and no work yet has been rich or deep enough to do justice to its reality. Nor is there any profound general debate on the subject. What is it? What does it mean to us? It transcends a given time and a given place. It offers us a chance to look into the darkest depths of the human soul.

My great-uncle, Xu Chi, a modernist poet in the 1930s, committed suicide in 1997. What made him wait 80 years before taking the jump? There was much speculation about his motives, but I have never doubted one comment attributed to him: 'I deeply regret the choice I made between the Modernist Movement and the Communist Party in the 1930s.' In the 1930s there was an attempt to bring in communism by 'westernising' the country: the West was 'more scientific' and 'more progressive' and this was 'the best of the West'. But when the Cold War ended, it was obvious that history had made a mockery of us. So many people realised their lives had been based on a lie. Had they been deceived, or had they, far worse, deceive others? It wasn't until history had turned full circle that they understood. After half a century of revolution and the 'transformation of traditional Chinese culture',

culture was in a worse state than ever. The communists destroyed the solid framework of traditional Chinese culture and were unable to transplant western culture into China. The worst of both cultures was united under the badge of 'Experience'. 'Modern transformation' is a fine phrase, but just another dirty lie. Chinese artists profit from 'politics' and consider themselves 'post-modern'. Essentially, they are 'pre-modern', and not because of some bad choice, but because they decided on this course. Compared to Xu Chi and those like him, they lack integrity and consequently the mud of communist culture sticks.

Home was more familiar when I could not return. I have 'returned home' and I feel more like a stranger than ever before. Or should I say that I am travelling incognito? Even when I am most at ease, sitting and talking with friends by lamplight, I know that in their eyes I am a person they knew 10 years ago. But they cannot imagine my life since then and there is an invisible gap. Daily I ask myself what the point of writing is? It is a question that returns to fundamental issues, to the value of thought and the joy of writing; a question that is irrelevant in China today. I returned, and to understand how painful and joyous it is, I have to put myself back in the shoes of someone who 'cannot return'. No wonder the poet Guo Lusheng, who sees his voluntary sojourn in a psychiatric institution as an escape, shouts excitedly, 'People who return have a lot in common with psychiatric patients!'

When Beijing's security police notice I am visiting 'my' old home, they install 24-hour surveillance outside, just as they did 10 years before. Disgusted, and a little wary, I leave the small, dusty room that has traversed my dreams as I was hurled about the four corners of the globe. It is a 'House of the Spirits' in the true sense and will remain with me forever. How I would love to have no memory. I walk around while the lorry carrying my books speeds down the highway. The Western Mountains recede into the background, a silhouette I have trusted since I was very young. How strange: such deep grey in the early evening dusk of winter. I think: I am looking on you for the last time. ❏

Yang Lian is a Chinese poet living in London. He has most recently been a co-editor of the 1998 anthology of Chinese poetry, a successor to the underground magazine Modern Chinese Poetry that published from 1990 to 1996. The book was banned in China in June this year